RAYS OF THE
ONE LIGHT

RAYS OF THE ONE LIGHT

WEEKLY COMMENTARIES ON THE BIBLE AND THE BHAGAVAD GITA

SWAMI KRIYANANDA

(J. DONALD WALTERS)

Printed in USA
First printing 1996
Revised fourth edition 2007

ISBN13: 978-1-56589-208-8
eISBN: 978-1-56589-524-9

Cover painting by Sandro da Verscio

Cover and interior design by Nayaswami Nirmala Schuppe

Library of Congress Cataloging-in-Publication Data

Walters, J. Donald.
 Rays of the one light: weekly commentaries on the Bible and the
Bhagavad Gita / Swami Kriyananda. — Rev. 4th ed.
  p.cm.
 ISBN 978-1-56589-208-8 (trade paper, weekly readings)
  1. Bible—Meditations. 2. Bhagavad Gita—Meditations. I. Title.
 BS491.5.W35 2007
 220.6—dc22

                                        2006103451

www.crystalclarity.com
800-424-1055
clarity@crystalclarity.com

CONTENTS

PREFACE

The chapters in this book, called "Weeks," were written to be read every week at the Sunday morning services at the Ananda churches of Self-Realization. They can also be read, of course, at any other time, and by individuals as well as by groups. They are universal, not sectarian, in their teaching, and are meant to be both instructive and inspiring for people of every, or of no, faith.

An attempt has been made to show the underlying unity between the Bible and the Bhagavad Gita, particularly, but also by implication the essential thread of unity that runs through all the great scriptures.

A visitor once asked Paramhansa Yogananda, in my presence, "Since you have called your church a 'church of all religions,' why do you concentrate primarily on the Bible and the Bhagavad Gita?"

"That was the wish of Babaji, the guru of my guru's guru," Yogananda replied. It is enough to demonstrate the ocean's depth by sounding it at one or two points. Its depth elsewhere can then be assumed.

At the Heart of Silence— the Eternal Word

Truth is one and eternal. Realize oneness with it in your deathless Self, within.

The following commentary is based on the teachings of Paramhansa Yogananda.

In the Gospel of St. John, Chapter 1, these immortal lines appear:

> *In the beginning was the Word, and the Word was with God, and the Word was God. The same was in the beginning with God. All things were made by him; and without him was not any thing made that was made. In him was life; and the life was the light of men. And the light shineth in darkness; and the darkness comprehended it not.*

Human vision beholds individuality and separation everywhere. Divine vision beholds the oneness of cosmic vibration, of which all things, no matter how diverse, are manifestations. Cosmic Sound— the "Word" of God—and Cosmic Light: These are eternal. The world, as revealed to us by our senses, is illusory.

In *Autobiography of a Yogi,* Paramhansa Yogananda relates an early experience he received of the divine aspect of reality:

> Sitting on my bed one morning, I fell into a deep reverie.
>
> "What is behind the darkness of closed eyes?" This probing thought came powerfully into my mind. An immense flash of light at once manifested to my inward gaze. Divine shapes of saints, sitting in meditation posture in mountain caves, formed like miniature cinema pictures on the large screen of radiance within my forehead.
>
> "Who are you?" I spoke aloud.
>
> "We are the Himalayan yogis." The celestial response is difficult to describe; my heart was thrilled.
>
> "Ah, I long to go to the Himalayas and become like you!" The vision vanished, but the silvery beams expanded in ever-widening circles to infinity.
>
> "What is this wondrous glow?"
>
> "I am Iswara. I am Light." The voice was as murmuring clouds.
>
> "I want to be one with Thee!"
>
> Out of the slow dwindling of my divine ecstasy, I salvaged a permanent legacy of inspiration to seek God.

Wise are we if we meditate on that experience of Yogananda's, and salvage from it even a breath of his inspiration. For, quite simply, there *is* nothing else! As the Bhagavad Gita says in the seventh Chapter:

> *I make and unmake this universe. Apart from Me nothing exists, O Arjuna. All things, like the beads of a necklace, are strung together on the thread of My consciousness, and are sustained by Me.*

Thus, through holy scripture, God has spoken to mankind.

Week 2

DID GOD CREATE THE UNIVERSE—OR BECOME IT?

Truth is one and eternal. Realize oneness with it in your deathless Self, within.

The following commentary is based on the teachings of Paramhansa Yogananda.

The Gospel of St. John, Chapter 1, contains a passage that explains the essential truth that creation is a process of *becoming*. The universe is not separate from God the Creator, but a part of Him even as our own dream-creations, during sleep, are figments of our consciousness. God's is the life; God's, the reality. Not a melody could be composed, not a poem written, were the melody and the poem not already there, simply waiting to be expressed.

In him was life; and the life was the light of men. And the light shineth in darkness; and the darkness comprehended it not.

Ego-directed desire is like static; it distorts the radioed messages of Infinity. But the pristine impulse from the divine, undistorted by limitation and delusion, is the life that gives rise to all that is. As the seventh Chapter of the Bhagavad Gita states:

> *I am the fluidity of water. I am the silver light of the moon and the golden light of the sun. I am the AUM chanted in all the Vedas: the Cosmic Sound moving as if soundlessly through the ether. I am the manliness of men. I am the good sweet smell of the moist earth. I am the luminescence of fire; the sustaining life of all living creatures. I am self-offering in those who would expand their little lives into cosmic life. O Arjuna, know Me as the eternal seed of all creatures. In the perceptive, I am their perception. In the great, I am their greatness. In the glorious, it is I who am their glory.*

Thus, through holy scripture, God has spoken to mankind.

Is God Present Even There, Where There Is Ignorance?

Truth is one and eternal. Realize oneness with it in your deathless Self, within.

The following commentary is based on the teachings of Paramhansa Yogananda.

The Gospel of St. John, Chapter 1, makes a reference to the divine light that is obscure to the rational faculty, but that enlightens our higher nature: *"The light shineth in darkness, and the darkness comprehended it not."* Reason recoils from this statement with innumerable questions. What is this darkness? Is it conscious, that it should comprehend anything? What sort of light would be capable of shining in darkness without transforming at least that part of the darkness in which it shines into light? Does this light shine only at night? And if so, why only then?

The solution is that, to divine sight, even daylight seems darkness. The sun itself, like the moon which shines only by reflected light from the sun, is but a kind of reflection of the cosmic light, which, being immaterial, is invisible to the eyes but which is the Great Source of all material reality.

In *Autobiography of a Yogi,* Paramhansa Yogananda describes his youthful visit to Ram Gopal Muzumdar, the "sleepless saint," who lived in the vision of that hidden light. "Around midnight," Yogananda wrote,

> Ram Gopal fell into silence, and I lay down on my blankets. Closing my eyes, I saw flashes of lightning; the vast space within me was a chamber of molten light. I opened my eyes and observed the same dazzling radiance. The room became a part of the infinite vault which I beheld with interior vision.
>
> "Why don't you go to sleep?"
>
> "Sir, how can I sleep in the presence of lightning, blazing whether my eyes are shut or open?"
>
> "You are blessed to have this experience; the spiritual radiations are not easily seen."
>
> The saint added a few words of affection.

This is the "light that shineth in darkness." It has been described variously in the great scriptures. In the Bhagavad Gita, the eleventh Chapter, the devotee, Arjuna, is given an experience of the infinite state and exclaims in awe:

> *If there should rise suddenly within the skies*
> *Sunburst of a thousand suns*
> *Flooding earth with beams undeemed-of,*
> *Then might be that Holy One's*
> *Majesty and radiance dreamed of!*

Thus, through holy scripture, God has spoken to mankind.

Week 4

The Infinite Christ

Truth is one and eternal. Realize oneness with it in your deathless Self, within.

The following commentary is based on the teachings of Paramhansa Yogananda.

The Gospel of St. John contains some of the most profound spiritual teachings in the Bible. In the first Chapter many subtle truths are suggested concerning higher stages of Self-realization.

Here, John the Baptist is described as one reaching up toward that high state. *"He was not that light,"* the Gospel tells us, *"but was sent to bear witness of that light."* Jesus Christ, by contrast, is described as the light itself. *"That was the true light, which lighteth every man that cometh into the world. He was in the world, and the world was made by him, and the world knew him not."*

One essential truth stands out in this teaching: that Jesus came not to dogmatize people with a new teaching, but to bring them timeless, universal truths. Disciples saw the master clothed in human form, and therefore judged him in terms of his greatness *relative* to the greatness of other teachers.

Wisdom, however, sees the master's very greatness in terms of a cosmic unity.

There is a passage in *The Path,* by Swami Kriyananda, in which this point is emphasized. The Master, Paramhansa Yogananda, explained,

> "The saint who attains that exalted consciousness never says, 'I am God,' for he sees it was the vast Ocean that became his little wave of ego. The wave, in other words, would not claim, when referring to the little self, to be the Ocean."

At this juncture Debi, who was present, cried excitedly, "But Sir, if you are one with that Ocean, that means you are God!"

"Why *I?*" Master asked. "Say *'He.'* He is God."

"But still, Sir, you are one with Him, and He is the only reality. That means *you,* too, are God."

"But this body isn't God!"

"You aren't identified with your body, Sir, so one may still say that you are God."

"Well, in that case why do you say, 'You'? *You,* too, are that! In a discussion of this sort, it is less confusing if we say, 'He.'"

"But what's the difference?"

"The scriptures say . . ." Master began.

"It's only your humility, Sir," Debi broke in, "that makes you distinguish between yourself and Him."

"How can there be humility, when there is no consciousness of ego?"

Triumphantly Debi cried, "But if you have no ego left, that means you *are* God!"

Master laughingly continued the earlier statement, which Debi had interrupted: "The scriptures say, 'He who knows Brahma becomes Brahma.'"

"There!" cried Debi. "You said it yourself!"

Master rejoined, still laughingly, "*I* didn't say it. It's the scriptures that say so." Master, in other words, would not identify those words with the human body speaking them. It was in his overarching spirit that he saw himself one with the Infinite. But Debi was unable to make this mental leap from a pure expression of Infinity to Infinity Itself.

"You quoted those scriptures, Sir," he reminded Master relentlessly. "That means you agree with them!"

Recognizing that the distinction was, perhaps, too subtle for many to grasp, Master concluded, "Well, he who says he *is* God, isn't God. And," he added with a smile, "he who says he isn't, isn't!"

And there the subject rested, amid general laughter.

The greater a spiritual teaching, the more greatly we betray it by particularizing it with dogmas.

Truth itself, not the Christian truth or the Hindu truth, incarnates on earth with the birth of a fully liberated master. As the Bhagavad Gita teaches in the fourth Chapter:

> *Unborn, changeless, Lord of Creation and controller of My cosmic nature though I am, yet entering Nature I am dressed in the cosmic garment of My own maya (delusion).*
>
> *O Bharata, whenever virtue declines and vice predominates, I incarnate on earth. Taking visible form, I come to destroy evil and re-establish virtue.*

Thus, through holy scripture, God has spoken to mankind.

THE MYSTERY OF AVATARA, OR DIVINE INCARNATION

Truth is one and eternal. Realize oneness with it in your deathless Self, within.

The following commentary is based on the teachings of Paramhansa Yogananda.

The Bhagavad Gita in the fourth Chapter states, as we saw last week:

> *O Bharata, whenever virtue declines and vice predominates, I incarnate on earth. Taking visible form, I come to destroy evil and re-establish virtue.*

What is the mystery of this divine manifestation? Great avatars, such as Krishna and Jesus Christ, are born as babies even as we all are. They take human form, and go through normal human experiences as they grow from childhood to adulthood. They eat. They play. They may seem to suffer sickness and disappointment like the rest of us. In what way are they different from other human beings?

The important thing to understand is that, even as they are like us, so are we also like them. Their realization can be ours, too. They come on earth to show us our own divine potential.

The difference lies not in the manner of their manifestation on earth, but in the consciousness with which they are born. All things are condensations, so to speak, of the Cosmic Vibration—AUM, described by St. John's Gospel as the Word. Most human beings, however, are unconscious of their divine origin. The avatars, on the other hand, come consciously as manifestations of that divine reality.

As the Gospel says in the first Chapter:

And the Word was made flesh, and dwelt among us, (and we beheld his glory, the glory as of the only begotten of the Father,) full of grace and truth.

Thus, through holy scripture, God has spoken to mankind.

Week 6

THE IMPORTANCE OF SOUL-RECEPTIVITY

Truth is one and eternal. Realize oneness with it in your deathless Self, within.

The following commentary is based on the teachings of Paramhansa Yogananda.

Chapter 1 of the Gospel of St. John states:

> *But as many as received him, to them gave he power to become the sons of God, even to them that believe on his name.*

This was a passage Paramhansa Yogananda often quoted to his disciples. "Be in tune," he would tell them. "Delusion can't touch you, if you will keep in tune."

"A few of you will fall," he said once. "But it needn't be, if you would stay in tune."

Of a disciple who became highly advanced, even though she didn't meditate much, he said, "She got there by attunement."

To one who found meditation difficult, he said, "I will meditate for you, as long as you stay in tune."

Truth is a state of consciousness, not a well-worded definition. It is in that consciousness, above all, that our lives are transformed. Therefore the Bhagavad Gita says, in the tenth Chapter:

To those who are ever attached to Me, and who worship Me with love, I impart discernment, by means of which they attain Me.

Out of My love for them, I, the Divine within them, set alight in them the radiant lamp of wisdom, thereby dispelling the darkness of their ignorance.

Thus, through holy scripture, God has spoken to mankind.

Week 7

THE LAW IS PERFECTED IN LOVE

Truth is one and eternal. Realize oneness with it in your deathless Self, within.

The following commentary is based on the teachings of Paramhansa Yogananda.

In the Gospel of St. John, Chapter 1, we read:

The law was given by Moses, but grace and truth came by Jesus Christ.

Grace means the power to rise, spiritually. Truth means the *experience* of divine realities, not the application in the outer world of that inner experience.

Divine love is the soul's *experience* of oneness with God. Kindness is the human *manifestation* of that love. Grace is deeper than mere kindness.

Wisdom is a divine *experience*. Justice to all is a human law, though divinely inspired. It follows as a consequence of the experience of wisdom. Truth goes deeper than mere justice.

While following the law, we should strive always to trace it back to its origins in the vision of God.

Therefore Krishna in the Bhagavad Gita urges the devotee not to be satisfied with spiritual precepts alone, but to go beyond them to the direct, inner experience of truth. In the eighteenth Chapter of that great scripture he says:

> *Nay! but once more*
> *Take My last word, My utmost meaning*
>   *have!*
> *Precious thou art to Me; right well beloved!*
> *Listen! I tell thee for thy comfort this.*
> *Give Me thy heart! adore Me! serve Me!*
>   *cling*
> *In faith and love and reverence to Me!*
> *So shalt thou come to Me! I promise true,*
> *For thou art sweet to Me!*
>   *And let go those—*
> *Rites and writ duties! Fly to me alone!*
> *Make Me thy single refuge! I will free*
> *Thy soul from all its sins! Be of good cheer!*

Thus, through holy scripture, God has spoken to mankind.

Week 8

CAN MAN SEE GOD?

Truth is one and eternal. Realize oneness with it in your deathless Self, within.

The following commentary is based on the teachings of Paramhansa Yogananda.

There is a saying in Chapter 1 of the Gospel of St. John that would seem to respond with a definite *No* to the question, Can man see God? The saying is:

No man hath seen God at any time; the only begotten Son, which is in the bosom of the Father, he hath declared him.

Many great saints, however, claim to have seen God. If we ask, then, "Can God be seen?" rather than, "Can *man* see God?" the answer is, "Yes! Else those saints lied. and the scriptures themselves lied." For Jesus also said, "Blessed are the pure in heart, for they shall see God."

The point is, it is not *man*—this human body, these human eyes—that sees God. God can be seen only with spiritual vision—with the eye of the soul.

As the Bhagavad Gita puts it in the eleventh Chapter:

"Thou canst not see Me with mortal eyes. Therefore I now give thee sight divine. Behold My supreme power of Yoga!"

With these words Hari, the exalted Lord of Yoga, revealed himself to Arjuna in His infinite form.

Paramhansa Yogananda, in *Autobiography of a Yogi,* describes the supernal experience in words more readily comprehensible to modern minds than the poetic phraseology of the Bhagavad Gita. The chapter "An Experience in Cosmic Consciousness" is one of the most inspiringly beautiful in all mystical literature. Here is a brief excerpt:

An oceanic joy broke upon calm endless shores of my soul. The Spirit of God, I realized, is exhaustless Bliss; His body is countless tissues of light.

[I saw] the divine dispersion of rays pour from an Eternal Source, blazing into galaxies, transfigured with ineffable auras. Again and again I saw the creative beams condense into constellations, then resolve into sheets of transparent flame. By rhythmic reversion, sextillion worlds passed into diaphanous luster; fire became firmament.

I cognized the center of the empyrean as a point of intuitive perception in my heart. Irradiating splendor issued from my nucleus to every part of the universal structure. . . . The creative voice of God I heard resounding as *AUM,* the vibration of the Cosmic Motor.

This, so the great masters aver, is what God is. And this also, they insist, is what we are in our deepest reality.

Thus, through holy scripture, God has spoken to mankind.

Week 9

By Thinking Can We Arrive at Understanding?

Truth is one and eternal. Realize oneness with it in your deathless Self, within.

The following commentary is based on the teachings of Paramhansa Yogananda.

There are many places in the Gospels where we see Jesus in open conflict with the Pharisees—that is to say, with man-made as opposed to true, mystical tradition. In the Gospel of St. Matthew, Chapter 15, we see a good example of how they and he "locked horns."

> *Then some of the scribes and Pharisees from Jerusalem came and asked Jesus, "Why do your disciples break our ancient tradition and eat their food without washing their hands properly first?"*

Jesus, after scolding them for their hypocrisy in observing lesser rules so carefully while ignoring the much more important ones, said,

> *"Listen, and understand this thoroughly!*

*It is not what goes **into** a man's mouth that
makes him common or unclean. It is what
comes **out** of a man's mouth that makes
him unclean."*

It wasn't that Jesus counseled against such whole-
some practices as washing one's hands before eat-
ing. In an age, however, when lesser rules were
given too much importance relative to the truly important observances—cleansing the heart of impure
desires, for example—he emphasized the supreme
importance of loving God and of communing with
Him.

The Pharisees—the orthodox religionists of his
day, in other words—had brought true religion
down to a level of intellectual hair-splitting. They
mistakenly considered the way to understanding to
lie through a minefield of definitions, which they
tried to refine to ultimate exactitude. Jesus taught,
however, that the intellect alone can never lead
one to truth. Without love, indeed, there *is* no ultimate verity. Without fixity of purpose, born of the
heart's devotion, the intellect wanders endlessly. It
cannot settle for long on anything. As the Bhagavad
Gita says in the second Chapter:

> *The intellects of those who lack fixity
> of spiritual purpose are inconstant, their
> interests endlessly ramified.*

Thus, through holy scripture, God has spoken to
mankind.

Dogmatism vs. Common Sense

Truth is one and eternal. Realize oneness with it in your deathless Self, within.

The following commentary is based on the teachings of Paramhansa Yogananda.

In the Gospel of St. Matthew, Chapter 7, Jesus warns:

> *Beware of false prophets, which come to you in sheep's clothing, but inwardly they are ravening wolves. Ye shall know them by their fruits. Do men gather grapes of thorns, or figs of thistles? Even so every good tree bringeth forth good fruit; but a corrupt tree bringeth forth evil fruit.*
>
> *A good tree cannot bring forth evil fruit, neither can a corrupt tree bring forth good fruit. Wherefore by their fruits ye shall know them.*

Jesus here, as indeed many times during his teaching, counsels people to use their God-given common sense, and not to rely on high-flown but undemonstrable claims. Common sense goes beyond abstract reason, for it is rooted in actual experience.

Even common sense, however, is deficient when the judgment called for goes *beyond* sensory experience. Ultimately, what he emphasized always, therefore, was *intuitive perception.*

Thus, he expected more of his disciples than crude common sense, and often scolded them for being too literal-minded—as he did, elsewhere, when they thought his statement, "I have meat to eat that you know not of," meant that he had steaks or sandwiches secreted about his person. His reference, of course, was to spiritual, not material, substance.

Words, even though appearing in the scriptures, are no substitute for direct perception of truth. Therefore the Bhagavad Gita says, in the second Chapter:

> *The sage who knows God has as little need for the scriptures as one might have for a pond when the whole land is covered in flood.*

Thus, through holy scripture, God has spoken to mankind.

REASON VS. INTUITION

Truth is one and eternal. Realize oneness with it in your deathless Self, within.

The following commentary is based on the teachings of Paramhansa Yogananda.

Jesus, when addressing his critics, appealed to reason and common sense. In his training of the disciples, however, he, like all great masters, encouraged in them the development of a higher faculty: soul-intuition. For it is only by intuition that spiritual perceptions are achieved.

In Chapter 16 of the Gospel of St. Matthew we find Jesus drawing on the intuition of his disciples by asking them who they thought he was, in reality. They immediately understood that what he wanted from them was a subtle answer, not some obvious reply based on his nationality, sex, and the like. Peter it was, at last, who understood and answered the question on its intended level: the spiritual.

> *"Thou art the Christ,"* he said, *"the son of the living God."*
> *And Jesus turned to him, saying, "Blessed art thou, Simon, son of Jonah: for not by*

human nature was this truth revealed to thee, but by my heavenly Father. And I tell thee this also: Thou art Peter, which is to say, a rock, and upon this rock will I build my church, and never will the powers of darkness overwhelm it."

Jesus was pleased with his disciple for relating to the question on its deepest level. Reason could not have given Peter that answer. The answer came through the faculty of soul intuition, and proved him thereby to be a spiritually advanced disciple. It was his intuitive perception—that insight which cannot be shaken by tempests of reasonable doubt—that Jesus praised in referring to him as a rock. The "church" he referred to, next, was the edifice of cosmic consciousness. Any outer church institution would have to depend, as in fact the Christian churches have always done, on the level of understanding of its individual leaders and members. Peter's intuitive perceptions could never have been passed on to an outward succession of prelates.

Clarity comes by direct soul-perception. Confusion results from excessive dependence on reason as the guide to understanding. As the second Chapter of the Bhagavad Gita states:

When your intellect, at present confused by the diversity of teaching in the scriptures, becomes steadfast in the ecstasy of deep meditation, then you will achieve final union with God.

Thus, through holy scripture, God has spoken to mankind.

WE ARE CHILDREN OF THE LIGHT

Truth is one and eternal. Realize oneness with it in your deathless Self, within.

The following commentary is based on the teachings of Paramhansa Yogananda.

It is common for people to perceive themselves according to their present realities. A person in ill health says, "I am ill." Few say, "I am well; it is my body that is suffering." People in a low income bracket say, "I am poor." Only the unusual person will say, "Though outwardly I live in poverty, inwardly I am wealthy."

Thus, when it comes to moral and spiritual development, people commonly identify themselves with their weaknesses and their mistakes. They consider it almost a sign of humility to say, "I am a sinner," though in effect what this means is that they identify themselves with their sinfulness, not with the soul's power to transcend all limitations in God.

The great masters, including Jesus Christ, have always emphasized the divine potential of mankind. To encourage us, they address us as children of light, not of darkness.

The Bible, in the Gospel of St. John, Chapter 3, makes the point that our true home is not the mud of this Earth, but the light of heaven. *"No man hath ascended up to heaven,"* it tells us, *"but him that came down from heaven."* This passage continues: *"[even so] the Son of man who is in heaven,"* emphasizing that Jesus, though he lived on earth, is perceived by the eye of wisdom as conscious, even in human form, of his true reality in heavenly spheres.

The way to know God is to live in godly consciousness, and not to bewail our imperfection and our distance from God. Jesus said, *"Blessed are the pure in heart, for they shall see God."* And the Bhagavad Gita states,

> *Seekers of union with the Lord find Him dwelling in their own hearts. But those who, lacking in wisdom, seek Him with impure motives, cannot perceive Him however much they struggle to do so.*

"If you want to know God," Paramhansa Yogananda said, "live in the thought that you have Him already."

Thus, through holy scripture, God has spoken to mankind.

Week 13

DEEDS VS. INTENTIONS

Truth is one and eternal. Realize oneness with it in your deathless Self, within.

The following commentary is based on the teachings of Paramhansa Yogananda.

Jesus Christ emphasized repeatedly the spirit, not the letter, of the law. In Chapter 5 of the Gospel of St. Matthew he speaks of the sin of killing, and of the legal punishment attendant on that sin, but says that more important than the act is the *desire* to kill, or to do harm. He shows that the sin of harmful *desire* goes beyond merely wanting to kill.

> *"My message to you,"* he said, *"is this: Whoever is angry with his brother without cause already stands condemned; whoever contemptuously calls his brother a fool shall answer for it to the Supreme Council; and whoever calls his brother an outcast of God shall be in danger of hellfire."*

"Brother," here, means any other human being. For all of us in the highest sense are brothers and sisters—children of our one Father-Mother, God.

The true self of one is the Self of all. To hurt another is, even if one doesn't realize it, to hurt oneself.

Swami Kriyananda in *The Path* recalls an episode in which the Master, Paramhansa Yogananda, revealed his sense of identity even with the plants. "One day," Kriyananda wrote, "we were moving a delicate but rather heavy tropical plant into position on the hillside. Our handling evidently was too rough, for Master cried out, 'Be careful what you are doing. Can't you *feel*? It's alive!'"

To wish death to anyone—to wish even harm to another creature—is to deny in oneself the reality of that divine life of which all of us are manifestations. It is, in short, to deny the eternal truth, proclaimed by the Bhagavad Gita in the second Chapter:

> *This Self is never born, nor does it perish.*
> *Once existing, it cannot ever cease to be. It*
> *is birthless, eternal, changeless, ever itself.*
> *It is not slain when the body is slain.*

Thus, through holy scripture, God has spoken to mankind.

Introduction to
Weeks 14 and 15

For those who are studying this book by the week, particularly for reading at Sunday services, this chapter and the next may be inserted wherever Palm Sunday and Easter occur.

Week 14
(Palm Sunday)

WHO IS THIS SON OF MAN?

Truth is one and eternal. Realize oneness with it in your deathless Self, within.

The following commentary is based on the teachings of Paramhansa Yogananda.

On Palm Sunday, the throng joyfully acclaimed Jesus Christ as he entered Jerusalem, casting palm fronds before him and singing, *"Hosanna! Blessed is he who comes in the name of the Lord! The Lord bless the king of Israel!"* (John 12:13)

Jesus Christ had told the people, *"The son of man must be lifted up."* His reference — so we are told — was to the mode of his impending crucifixion. Some persons on that occasion had asked, *"Who is this son of man?"*

Was Jesus a human being, merely? Those who, on Palm Sunday, called him king little realized the actual nature of his kingdom. He was far more than what they imagined. Yes, of course he ate, drank, walked, slept, and talked like others. His consciousness, however, was centered in infinity. Yes — again — he laughed like others: But his laughter expressed divine joy, not mere merriment.

Again, he wept like them: But never with human grief. The tears he shed were for the sufferings of unenlightened human beings: Never were they shed in self-pity.

Jesus Christ was wakeful in God. Most people, by contrast, are asleep spiritually.

How strange to reflect that less than a week from that entry into Jerusalem — so joyfully acclaimed — he would be arrested, condemned, and crucified! Such is the bitter-sweetness of human existence: smiles of welcome one day — insults, even persecution the next. How few realize that Christ's suffering would not be for himself, but for people's ignorance — for those who had not yet understood the deeper reality that dwelt also in them!

Everyone is born "trailing clouds of glory," as the poet Wordsworth put it. Even the meanest beggar has lived a story, or will eventually have lived it, more magnificent than the greatest epic ever written.

In the Bhagavad Gita, this dichotomy between the "son of man" and the inner "Son of God" is beautifully described. Sri Krishna, representing God in human form, reveals his true nature in infinity. In the eleventh chapter of that great scripture, his chief disciple Arjuna exclaims:

> *O Infinite Light!*
> *Thy radiance, spreading o'er the universe,*
> *Shines into the very darkest abyss!*
> *Thy voice o'erwhelms the roar of cosmic*
> *   cataclysms!*

Lo! the myriad stars are Thy diadem;
Thy scepter radiates power everywhere!
O Immortal Brahman, Lord of all:
Again and again at Thy feet of Infinity
I lie in prostration before Thee!

Thus, through holy scripture, God has spoken to mankind.

RESURRECTION FOR
EVERY SOUL

Truth is one and eternal. Realize oneness with it in your deathless Self, within.

The following commentary is based on the teachings of Paramhansa Yogananda.

In the Gospel of St. John, Chapter 20, we read the inspiring account of Jesus' resurrection:

> *The first day of the week cometh Mary Magdalene early, when it was yet dark, unto the sepulchre, and seeth the stone taken away from the sepulchre.*
>
> *Then she runneth, and cometh to Simon Peter, and to the other disciple, whom Jesus loved, and saith unto them, They have taken away the Lord! . . .*
>
> *Then the same day at evening, being the first day of the week, when the doors were shut where the disciples were assembled for fear of the Jews, came Jesus and stood in their midst, and saith unto them, Peace be unto you.*

The resurrection of Jesus, doubted by many but affirmed by those who were close to him, was a miraculous event, though one not unique in history. For many great saints of other religions have appeared to their disciples after death. Sometimes their appearances have been, as that of Jesus was, in flesh-and-blood form, and not only in vision.

Paramhansa Yogananda relates in *Autobiography of a Yogi* the account of his guru Sri Yukteswar's resurrection after his earthly passing. Miracles of this type are revealed only rarely to the masses, but accounts of them, related by men and women of reputed truthfulness, have inspired many devotees with faith in the reality of subtler-than-material states of existence.

Resurrection, Yogananda explained, means transformation, ultimately, from any lower state of being to a higher one. Worldly consciousness cannot imagine such transformation except in terms of, perhaps, an improvement of the present mess of potage with the addition of a new flavoring. Divine consciousness, however, is capable of taking the base metal of worldliness and transforming it into the spiritual gold of divine wisdom and love.

In keeping with this truth, the Bhagavad Gita, in the ninth Chapter, tells us:

> *Ah! ye who into this ill world are come—fleeting and false—set your faith fast on Me! Fix heart and thought on Me! Adore Me! Bring Offerings to Me! Make Me prostrations! Make Me your supremest joy!*

*and, undivided, unto My rest your spirits
shall be guided.*

Thus, through holy scripture, God has spoken to
mankind.

To Each According to His Faith

Truth is one and eternal. Realize oneness with it in your deathless Self, within.

The following commentary is based on the teachings of Paramhansa Yogananda.

In the Gospel of St. John, Chapter 3, we read:

> *Everyone that doeth evil hateth the light, neither cometh to the light, lest his deeds should be reproved. But he that doeth truth cometh to the light, that his deeds may be made manifest, that they are wrought in God.*

It is a common experience, shared by most people, that when a person errs he experiences a desire to hide that error from his conscience instead of holding it up for purification. Error clutches its misdeeds to itself, and resists correction, though it is only in the state of purity that we can achieve perfect freedom. It requires an act of will to offer that awareness up to the light, and to hold it there until one's inner darkness is completely dissipated.

For every state of consciousness has its own attractive power. And the more we allow that attraction to act upon us, the more we attract to ourselves the objective circumstances and experiences natural to it. Our faith is the attractive power of our underlying state of consciousness. Goodness attracts goodness; it takes goodness even to *see* goodness. Evil attracts evil, and it takes evil even to *see* evil— that is, to take special note of its existence.

Whatever there is in you of darkness or light, offer it up to the heights. In the Supreme Light alone will we find salvation. Accept nothing less in yourself as your lasting reality. As the Bhagavad Gita says, in the twelfth Chapter:

> *Cling thou to me!*
> *Clasp Me with heart and mind! So shalt*
> *   thou dwell*
> *Surely with Me on high. But if thy thought*
> *Droops from such height; if thou be'st weak*
> *   to set*
> *Body and soul upon Me constantly,*
> *Despair not! give Me lower service! seek*
> *To reach Me, worshiping with steadfast will;*
> *And, if thou canst not worship steadfastly,*
> *Work for Me, toil in works pleasing to Me!*
> *For he that laboureth right for love of Me*
> *Shall finally attain! But, if in this*
> *Thy faint heart fails, bring Me thy failure!*

Thus, through holy scripture, God has spoken to mankind.

How High Should We Aspire?

Truth is one and eternal. Realize oneness with it in your deathless Self, within.

The following commentary is based on the teachings of Paramhansa Yogananda.

The passage this week is from the Gospel of St. Matthew, Chapter 5:

> *I say unto you, That except your righteousness shall exceed the righteousness of the scribes and Pharisees, ye shall in no case enter into the kingdom of heaven.*

The easiest explanation for these words is that they were spoken in criticism of the scribes and Pharisees, particularly since Jesus was often verbally attacked by them, and stood up to them fearlessly. However, it wouldn't have been much of a challenge to the disciples, who aspired to spiritual perfection, to tell them, "Don't be like those who lack any such aspiration."

Jesus in fact says only a few verses later, "Be ye

therefore perfect, even as your Father which is in heaven is perfect."

What Jesus was referring to here, then, was the *self-* righteousness of the priests. Don't seek perfection, he was saying to his disciples, in the image you project toward others. Don't be satisfied with a goodness born merely of ego-definitions. The highest virtue is to transcend the very thought of personal virtue in the realization of God alone as the Doer. Before this realization, even the thought, "I am kind," or, "I am truthful," is self-limiting.

As it says in the Bhagavad Gita, the seventh Chapter:

> *Yet hard the wise Mahatma is to find,*
> *That man who sayeth, "All is Vasudev!"*

Thus, through holy scripture, God has spoken to mankind.

PERFECTION IS
SELF-TRANSCENDENCE

Truth is one and eternal. Realize oneness with it in your deathless Self, within.

The following commentary is based on the teachings of Paramhansa Yogananda.

We begin this week with a passage from the Gospel of St. Matthew, Chapter 5:

> *Love your enemies; bless them that curse you; do good to them that hate you; and pray for them which despitefully use you, and persecute you; . . .*
>
> *If ye love them which love you, what reward have ye? Do not even the tax collectors the same?*
>
> *And if ye salute your brethren only, what do ye more than others? Do not even pagans so?*
>
> *Be ye therefore perfect, even as your Father which is in heaven is perfect.*

This teaching is a continuation of last week's lesson. To love all equally is possible only by seeing

God everywhere—in others as well as in oneself. See whatever comes to you unasked for as a manifestation of His will. Be grateful for the pains you experience, for they are healing strokes of His love. Sometimes, healing is effected only by strong measures, but His love for you is manifested in the very attempt to heal.

Strive always to be impersonal, as though whatever happens to you were happening to someone else.

Persecution gives us the supreme opportunity to deny the thought, "This is happening to *me*," and to affirm our inner freedom from the thought of ego. Don't allow the negative perceptions of others to become your own self-definition.

Seek God: This is the true goal of life—though how difficult to cling to in the midst of hatred, spite, and persecution! The Bhagavad Gita tells us in the seventh Chapter:

> *Out of thousands, one strives for spiritual attainment; and out of many blessed true seekers, who strive assiduously to reach Me, one, perhaps, perceives Me as I am.*

O truth seeker, be one, among all those thousands, who seeks the supreme goal!

Thus, through holy scripture, God has spoken to mankind.

THE SECRET OF RIGHT ACTION

Truth is one and eternal. Realize oneness with it in your deathless Self, within.

The following commentary is based on the teachings of Paramhansa Yogananda.

One of the most famous stories in the Gospels is that of Martha and Mary. Jesus, visiting the home of Martha, was teaching while her sister Mary sat at his feet absorbing his divine love and wisdom. Martha, meanwhile, busied herself with serving her guests, and was upset with Mary for not helping her.

> *"Lord,"* she cried, *"doesn't it matter to you that my sister has left me to do all this serving alone? Please ask her to help me."*
>
> *"Martha, Martha,"* Jesus answered, *"thou art careful and troubled about many things.*
>
> *"But one thing is needful: and Mary hath chosen that good part, which shall not be taken away from her."*

This story is classic, for Martha's complaint is very understandable, and not, on the surface of it, spiritually wrong. Jesus may well have told Mary to get up and help her. We don't really know that he didn't, considerate as he always was of others' needs. But the *teaching* here doesn't concern the obvious dilemma of devotees: to work for God, or to spend all one's time in prayer. It concerns, rather, the attitude of the mind.

Jesus didn't tell Martha: "Martha, you are doing too much." He told her, rather, "You are letting your work affect your inner peace." *That* was the contrast: not work vs. contemplation, but restless preoccupation vs. peaceful absorption under all circumstances.

As it says in the Bhagavad Gita, the second Chapter:

> *Actions performed under the influence of desire are greatly inferior to those which are guided by wisdom. Happiness eludes people when they act from self-interest. Seek shelter, therefore, in the equanimity of wisdom.*

Thus, through holy scripture, God has spoken to mankind.

ACTIVITY VS. INNER COMMUNION

Truth is one and eternal. Realize oneness with it in your deathless Self, within.

The following commentary is based on the teachings of Paramhansa Yogananda.

Last week we contemplated the well-known story of Martha and Mary. Traditionally, this story has been offered to show the two classic approaches to salvation: the first, through action, and the second, through prayer. The excuse of the Marthas of this world has always been, "The church needs its Marthas, too." Treatises, moreover, have been written to justify the Martha approach to piety, praising her self-sacrifice as, perhaps, an even higher demonstration of devotion. (Thus do the unmeditative in religion try to justify themselves!) Yet the fact remains that Jesus rebuked Martha. Elsewhere, moreover, he spoke of the *virtue* of feeding the hungry, curing the sick, and housing those who were homeless. It wasn't that he disapproved of serving people.

Wrong *attitude* was the object of his criticism. What he was criticizing was forgetfulness of the true goal of right, spiritual action. Good deeds, outwardly, without inner communion with God, will result in good karma but will not bring final freedom from *all* karma.

The path to inner freedom was described by Paramhansa Yogananda in these words: "Be always calmly active, and actively calm."

As it says in the Bhagavad Gita, the second Chapter:

> *He who is not shaken by anxiety during times of sorrow, nor elated during times of happiness; who is free from egoic desires and their attendant fear and anger: Such an one is of steady discrimination.*

Do your duty in life—so counsels this great scripture elsewhere—but never lose sight of Him to whom all action should be dedicated.

Thus, through holy scripture, God has spoken to mankind.

Week 21

THE BEST WAY TO WORSHIP

Truth is one and eternal. Realize oneness with it in your deathless Self, within.

The following commentary is based on the teachings of Paramhansa Yogananda.

In Chapter 4 of the Gospel of St. John, the woman of Samaria asks Jesus, Where is the best place to worship? This question might be expanded to include: What is the best church? What is the best religion? Is it important to go on pilgrimage to holy shrines? What is the best ritual? What is the best mantra or prayer?

Jesus cut across all such questioning with his reply:

> *The hour cometh, and now is, when the true worshippers shall worship the Father in spirit and in truth: for the Father seeketh such to worship Him.*
>
> *God is a Spirit: and they that worship him must worship him in spirit and in truth.*

It was not that outer considerations of place,

church, ritual, etc., are irrelevant. Each person should find those practices and observances which are compatible with his own nature—one might say, with his own vibrations. Not everyone's natural path is the same. God sent different religions into the world to satisfy different human needs.

The overarching concern, however, considering that the goal is to find God, is to include in one's worship daily, inner communion with the Lord. God is Silence: He must be sought, therefore, in inner silence. God is Absolute Love: He must be sought, therefore, in the silence of love. God is Spirit, and thus immaterial: He must be sought, above all, in the expanding peace of deep meditation.

Thus, the Bhagavad Gita states in the sixth Chapter:

> *Sequestered should he sit,*
> *Steadfastly meditating, solitary,*
> *His thoughts controlled, his passions laid*
> *   away,*
> *From every craving for possession freed.*

Wherever you are, whatever your outward beliefs and observances, seek God in the silence of your own soul.

Thus, through holy scripture, God has spoken to mankind.

Week 22

THE INNER KINGDOM

Truth is one and eternal. Realize oneness with it in your deathless Self, within.

The following commentary is based on the teachings of Paramhansa Yogananda.

Most people imagine that the "inner kingdom," as Jesus described it, lacks the fascination they attribute to sense life: the bright lights, the diverse attractions, the joys and the laughter. Little do they realize what a vast universe exists in their own selves!

There are many passages in the Old and New Testaments of the Bible that describe aspects of this inner kingdom. In the Book of Genesis we read: *"And the Lord God planted a garden eastward in Eden. . . . And the tree of life also in the midst of the garden, and the tree of knowledge of good and evil"* (Genesis 2:8, 9). This garden was in no earthly place. It exists even now, in the very Self of every human being! The legend of Adam and Eve is allegorical. It describes how the first human beings dissipated their spiritual energy, centered in the spine. The spine is the channel through which flows the river of baptism and of spiritual life.

The Bhagavad Gita tells us, *"The wise speak of an eternal ashvatta tree, with its roots above and its branches below"* (15:1) The "tree of life," spoken of also in Genesis, is the spine. Its roots are above, in the brain's energy. Its branches are the outward spreading nervous system. When the "sap," which is to say, the energy, flows downward the consciousness is drawn into delusion. On the other hand, when the energy is drawn upward in deep meditation, the consciousness is drawn toward its eternal source, God, and is at last united with Him.

Krishna in the Bhagavad Gita therefore urges his chief disciple Arjuna to embrace the yoga science, the path of meditation. *"The yogi,"* he says, *"is greater than the ascetic, greater even than the followers of the paths of wisdom [Gyana Yoga] or of action [Karma Yoga]. Be thou, O Arjuna, a yogi!"*

For those who would find the divine truth, Krishna gives this description of the yogi:

> *Steadfast a lamp burns, sheltered from the*
> *wind;*
> *Steadfastly meditating, solitary,*
> *Such is the likeness of the Yogi's mind*
> *Shut from sense-storms and burning bright*
> *to heaven.*

Thus, through holy Scripture, God has spoken to mankind.

Why Do Devotees Fall?

Truth is one and eternal. Realize oneness with it in your deathless Self, within.

The following commentary is based on the teachings of Paramhansa Yogananda.

An endlessly fascinating question is, Why did Judas fall after receiving the extraordinary blessing of being accepted into the inner circle of Jesus Christ's disciples? For Judas was one of the twelve apostles. Yet he be-trayed Jesus, and earned for himself the opprobrium of Christendom for all futurity for his sin.

We find Judas reprimanding Jesus just days before that betrayal. Jesus, aware that his disciples would soon be facing, with his death, the supreme tragedy of their lives, allowed Mary to express her devotion by anointing his feet with costly ointment. This act of "wanton waste," as Judas saw it, awakened indignation in that disciple.

> "Why was not this ointment sold for three hundred pence, and given to the poor?"
>
> This he said, not that he cared for the

poor; but because he was a thief, and kept the purse, and bare what was put therein.

Then said Jesus, "Let her alone: against the day of my burying hath she kept this. For the poor always ye have with you: but me ye have not always."

Doubt not the power of delusion. Respect it—indeed, fear it, though not in the sense of cowering before it. For, as Yogananda said, "One is not safe until he attains *nirbikalpa samadhi*—the state of final union with God."

Judas, through attachment to money, opened his consciousness to subtle influences, which may be called satanic, that drew his thoughts toward other related attitudes: the importance of worldly power, for instance, and of worldly influence.

The Bhagavad Gita gives a graphic explanation of how easily the mind can be drawn downward, once it begins to feed on wrong attitudes. In the second Chapter, Sri Krishna states:

If one ponders on sense objects, there springs up attraction to them. From attraction grows desire. Desire, impatient for fulfillment, flames to anger. From anger there arises infatuation (the delusion that one object alone is worth clinging to, to the exclusion of all others). From infatuation ensues forgetfulness of the higher Self. From forgetfulness of the Self follows degeneration of the discriminative faculty.

And when discrimination is lost, there follows the annihilation of one's spiritual life.

"At the first thought of delusion," Paramhansa Yogananda said, "that is the time to stop it."

Thus, through holy scripture, God has spoken to mankind.

How Devotees Rise

Truth is one and eternal. Realize oneness with it in your deathless Self, within.

The following commentary is based on the teachings of Paramhansa Yogananda.

Last week we asked the question, Why do devotees fall? and we considered the downfall of Judas in this context. Jesus, in answer to Judas's criticism for allowing Mary to rub his feet with spikenard, a very costly ointment, said, *"The poor always ye have with you: but me ye have not always."*

Jesus is saying here that there is one supreme "injustice" that needs eradication: poverty, yes, but not of a material kind: poverty in a spiritual sense.

Divine blessings are not common in this world. They are extraordinary. When they come, we should give them priority above every other consideration.

Never allow a moment of inner joy, for instance, to be set aside for lesser "duties." Divine attunement is our *highest* priority. As Lahiri Mahasaya, the guru of Yogananda's guru, said, "To listen to the heart's inner sound (AUM, which issues from the very center of our being) is man's highest duty."

Mary, on this occasion, was not communing in inner silence with Christ's spirit, as she had been when Martha urged Jesus to reproach her for not helping out in the kitchen. Mary this time was serving outwardly, but in a very different spirit from the restless fussing for which Jesus had reprimanded her sister, Martha. Those who see a radical difference between the paths of action and meditation should understand this distinction. To serve in the right spirit is necessary, for only thereby can we overcome our karmic tendencies toward restless activity. The important thing is that that spirit be always inwardly focused: that in everything we do we act in loving service to the Lord.

Therefore the Bhagavad Gita says in the third Chapter:

The state of freedom from action [that is, of eternal rest in the Spirit] cannot be achieved without action. No one, by mere renunciation and outward non-involvement, can attain perfection.

Whenever the spirit of God descends upon you, however, remember the words of Jesus, "Me ye have not always with you."

Thus, through holy scripture, God has spoken to mankind.

THE ETERNAL NOW

Truth is one and eternal. Realize oneness with it in your deathless Self, within.

The following commentary is based on the teachings of Paramhansa Yogananda.

"When will I find God?" Many devotees have asked this question. Because worldly goals require time, usually, for their fulfillment, we imagine time to be a factor on the spiritual path. And so it is, but only because we *think* it is! God is as much with us now as He will ever be. It is not He who needs to come to us: *We* need to come to Him! And that process of coming is a matter of transforming our self-perception.

In the Gospel of St. John, Chapter 4, Jesus Christ says:

> *Say not ye, There are yet four months, and then cometh harvest? Behold, I say unto you, Lift up your eyes, and look on the fields; for they are white already to harvest.*

There is a practical teaching in these words, apart from their statement that we have God already, and have only to realize that truth. Jesus is saying, "Lift up your eyes and look. . . ." To hold the eyes uplifted is the best position for meditation. For the seat of superconsciousness lies at a point midway between the eyebrows—in the frontal lobe of the brain just behind that point. This point is known also as the Christ center. By lifting up your eyes and concentrating there, you will find it easier to enter the state of ecstasy. That is why saints in every religion have often been observed, during states of deep inner communion, with their eyes uplifted, focused on the inner light—"white," as Jesus said, "already to harvest."

The Bhagavad Gita goes further into this meditative teaching. In the sixth Chapter it states:

> *Holding the spine firm, the neck and head erect and motionless, let the yogi focus his eyes at the starting place of the nose [the point between the eyebrows]. Let not his gaze roam elsewhere.*

In meditation, tell yourself: "I have Him already! I am alive forever in the Divine Light."

Thus, through holy scripture, God has spoken to mankind.

Week 26

THE REDEEMING LIGHT

Truth is one and eternal. Realize oneness with it in your deathless Self, within.

The following commentary is based on the teachings of Paramhansa Yogananda.

The Book of Isaiah in the Bible, Chapter 9, tells us:

> *The people that walked in darkness have seen a great light: they that dwell in the land of the shadow of death, upon them hath the light shined.*

What is this light of which so many scriptures speak? In *Autobiography of a Yogi*, by Paramhansa Yogananda, we read of an early experience the Master had with that light:

> I was blessed about the age of eight with a wonderful healing through the photograph of Lahiri Mahasaya. This experience gave intensification to my [divine] love. While at our family estate in Ichapur, Bengal, I was stricken with Asiatic cholera. My life was despaired of; the doctors could do

nothing. At my bedside, Mother frantically motioned me to look at Lahiri Mahasaya's picture on the wall above my head.

"Bow to him mentally!" She knew I was too feeble even to lift my hands in salutation. "If you really show your devotion and inwardly kneel before him, your life will be spared!"

I gazed at his photograph and saw there a blinding light, enveloping my body and the entire room. My nausea and other uncontrollable symptoms disappeared; I was well. At once I felt strong enough to bend over and touch Mother's feet in appreciation of her immeasurable faith in her guru. Mother pressed her head repeatedly against the little picture.

"O Omnipresent Master, I thank thee that thy light hath healed my son!"

I realized that she too had witnessed the luminous blaze through which I had instantly recovered from a usually fatal disease.

"Where My light is," God once told a saint whom the divine light had healed, "no darkness can dwell." The divine light—pure, calm, liberating—is the only final cure for every kind of delusion: ill health, emotional grief, and spiritual ignorance. Seek it daily in the silence, in deep meditation.

As the Bhagavad Gita says in the fifth Chapter:

For whom
That darkness of the soul is chased by light,
Splendid and clear shines manifest the Truth
As if a Sun of Wisdom sprang to shed
Its beams of light.

Thus, through holy scripture, God has spoken to mankind.

ABIDING IN GOD

Truth is one and eternal. Realize oneness with it in your deathless Self, within.

The following commentary is based on the teachings of Paramhansa Yogananda.

Yogananda often emphasized—more often to his disciples than to the general public, but also to everyone generally, for it was a universal teaching—the importance of attunement. For divine understanding cannot be created: It must be perceived. To the disciples, Yogananda spoke of the importance of attunement with the guru. To others, he urged the importance at least of attuning oneself to higher consciousness. Can an eagle rise without support from the sustaining air?

Jesus Christ said in the Gospel of St. John, Chapter 15:

> I am the vine, ye are the branches: He that abideth in me, and I in him, the same bringeth forth much fruit: for without me ye can do nothing.
>
> If a man abide not in me, he is cast forth

*as a branch, and is withered; and men
gather them, and cast them into the fire,
and they are burned.*

*If ye abide in me, and my words abide in
you, ye shall ask what ye will, and it shall
be done unto you.*

*Herein is my Father glorified, that ye
bear much fruit; so shall ye be my disciples.*

How can we "abide in him"? Jesus says, "If my
words abide in you." By words he meant not only
his spoken words, but his vibrations, his consciousness, of which the words are only an expression.
We must abide by the teachings, but we must also
absorb those teachings into ourselves, that they
become our own experience. For disciples of this
path, the more, in their hearts, they live consciously
in the presence of the masters, the more they will
find the divine presence living within them.

And for all truth seekers, whether disciples or
not, the more they live sustained inwardly by the
awareness of God's presence, the higher they will
find themselves soaring in wisdom and joy.

For the Bhagavad Gita says, in the tenth Chapter:

*I am the Source of everything; from Me
all creation emerges. Blessed with this realization, the wise, awe-stricken, adore Me.*

Thus, through holy scripture, God has spoken to
mankind.

Self-Reliance vs. *Self*-Reliance

Truth is one and eternal. Realize oneness with it in your deathless Self, within.

The following commentary is based on the teachings of Paramhansa Yogananda.

Last week we considered the need for attunement—with God, with the gurus, with the wisdom of others—until we make that wisdom our own. There is a strong, and in fact valid, belief nowadays in the need for standing on one's own feet rather than depending weakly on others to carry us by their strength.

Swami Kriyananda was once asked, "What is the best yoga posture?" "That one," he replied, "which sets you squarely on your own two feet."

Our strength must come from within. If that strength comes from the ego, however, instead of from soul-consciousness, it is like a guitar string without its sounding board: the notes it emits will be thin and feeble. Our strength must come from within, but must be coupled with recognition of our inner link with broader and higher realities.

The Bhagavad Gita says in the tenth Chapter:

Everyone in this world whose life is glorious, or prosperous, or powerful—know that his achievement is but a little spark from the great sun of My effulgence.

Jesus in talking to his disciples emphasized also the power of attunement with his own consciousness as a ray of the Divine. For this ray had descended already, through him, in response to their devotion; it was a sign that God was already "listening" to them with receptive attention, and did not require to be wooed in that way any longer. In the passage preceding the one that we read last week, Jesus said:

I am the true vine, and my Father is the husbandman.

Every branch in me that beareth not fruit he taketh away: and every branch that beareth fruit, he purgeth it, that it may bring forth more fruit.

Now ye are clean through the word which I have spoken unto you.

Abide in me, and I in you. As the branch cannot bear fruit of itself, except it abide in the vine; no more can ye, except ye abide in me.

This was the meaning of Paramhansa Yogananda's counsel also, when speaking more intimately to the disciples of the need for attunement with him.

Thus, through holy scripture, God has spoken to mankind.

Week 29

SELF-EFFORT, TOO, IS NEEDED

Truth is one and eternal. Realize oneness with it in your deathless Self, within.

The following commentary is based on the teachings of Paramhansa Yogananda.

These past weeks we discussed the need for balancing self-effort with receptivity to divine grace. Both are important in the spiritual life. Passive dependence on grace hasn't the magnetism to attract grace. Boastful self-confidence, however, which closes itself off from the higher, divine power is shallow, brittle, and—given life's many uncertainties—susceptible to ultimate failure.

There is a story in the Bible that illustrates the need to put forth personal effort so as to draw magnetically on the divine power. The story occurs in the Gospel of St. Luke, Chapter 8:

> *But as he went, the crowds nearly suffocated him. Among them was a woman who had had a hemorrhage for twelve years and who had derived no benefit from anybody's treatment. She came up behind Jesus and touched the edge of his cloak. As a result, her hemorrhage stopped immediately.*

"Who was it who touched me?" Jesus asked.

When everybody denied it, Peter remonstrated,

"Master, the crowds are all round, pressing you on every side!"

But Jesus said, "Somebody touched me. I felt power going out from me."

When the woman realized that she had not escaped notice, she came forward trembling and fell at his feet, and admitted before everyone why she had touched him, adding that she had been instantaneously cured.

"Daughter," Jesus said, "It is by your faith that you have been healed. Go in peace."

Self-confidence and self-effort are necessary, as the ignition of a car is necessary to the motor. Of what use the ignition, however, if the motor itself will not work? Wise is he who recognizes the real power in the universe, and guides his life by that supreme power. As it says in the Bhagavad Gita, the ninth Chapter:

To those who meditate on Me as their Very Own, ever united to Me by incessant worship, I make good their deficiencies, and render permanent their gains.

Thus, through holy scripture, God has spoken to mankind.

Do You Need a Guru?

Truth is one and eternal. Realize oneness with it in your deathless Self, within.

The following commentary is based on the teachings of Paramhansa Yogananda.

Many people scoff at the idea of having a guru. True to human nature generally, they make a virtue of their scoffing. "*I* am responsible for what I do," they announce, "responsible for my mistakes as well as for my victories. What would I ever learn if I handed over my development to someone else? To depend on another for guidance would be an act of spiritual cowardice."

It would be understandable for someone gifted with some trivial ability, for instance with words, to insist on doing his crossword puzzle himself without letting anyone else help him. But supposing, even in such trivial matters, he had no such gift? What virtue would there be in refusing to learn? For that matter, moreover, where do our gifts come from? They are not a native ability. Still, crossword puzzles are hardly an important challenge. What if a person wanted to do something daring: to climb a cliff, for instance, but refused to study the art of mountain climbing? He would climb at the risk of his life.

And how much more is risked than physical life in the great adventure of the divine search, where the risk is to salvation itself! Where is the sacrifice in seeking guidance? Even a mountain guide wouldn't presume to do one's climbing for one; his purpose would be only to help the neophyte to climb safely. To have a wise guru is not a sign of weakness, but of plain common sense.

All the saints, aware as they are of the hazards of the adventure, agree on the importance of having a guide, or guru. And these are the heroes speaking, not cowards or spiritual weaklings.

Jesus emphasized the importance of having a teacher by asking John to baptize him. In the Gospel of St. Matthew, Chapter 3, we read of his coming to John. *"Thus,"* Jesus said to John, *"it becometh us to fulfill all righteousness."*

In the Bhagavad Gita, the fourth Chapter, Sri Krishna says:

> *Open thyself to those who have attained wisdom. They will be thy teachers. Ask questions of them [both verbally and mentally]. Serve them faithfully, and with devotion.*

How is the devotee to recognize one who has attained wisdom? The Bhagavad Gita gives us this inspiring description of the sage:

By this sign is he known,
Being of equal grace to comrades, friends,
Chance-comers, strangers, lovers, enemies,
Aliens and kinsmen; loving all alike,
Evil or good.

Thus, through holy scripture, God has spoken to mankind.

How Democratic Is Truth?

Truth is one and eternal. Realize oneness with it in your deathless Self, within.

The following commentary is based on the teachings of Paramhansa Yogananda.

We live in an age when people assume that knowledge should be available equally to all. In matters susceptible of judgment by normal common sense, however, everyone knows there are exceptions. Access to a control room for intercontinental missiles is limited, by universal consent, to a very few. Access to the controls of a passenger airliner is limited to those with the necessary knowledge for operating them, and also to those with the proper authorization. If people don't see the disadvantages of making more subtle knowledge universally available, it is only because they are ignorant of the risks involved.

In the case of subtle knowledge, the main disadvantage in making it universally available is the harm it might do to one who isn't ready for it, and who might even mock it. True, by mocking truth he might undermine the faith of a few truth seekers. But then, such tests can also be beneficial, as a means of strengthening faith. Again true, the clever doubter's misrepresentation of those truths may dissuade a few seekers from following the spiritual path. But if a seeker really is sincere, he will recognize the truth eventually because it resonates with his own being.

No, the greatest problem accrues to the shallow doubter himself. To give him an opportunity to affirm his ignorance might only estrange him even more from the truth, delaying the time when he will turn—as all people *must,* eventually—to the light.

Thus, the scriptures advise, not secrecy, but discretion in the sharing of truth. Jesus Christ says in the Gospel of St. Matthew, Chapter 7:

> *Give not that which is holy unto dogs, neither cast ye your pearls before swine, lest they trample them under their feet, and turn again and rend you.*

And Sri Krishna says in the eighteenth Chapter of the Bhagavad Gita:

> *Never speak of these truths to one who is without self-control or devotion, who renders no service, who does not care to hear, or who speaks ill of Me.*

Thus, through holy scripture, God has spoken to mankind.

DOES GOD HIDE THE TRUTH?

Truth is one and eternal. Realize oneness with it in your deathless Self, within.

The following commentary is based on the teachings of Paramhansa Yogananda.

In last week's reading we saw that the great masters themselves counsel discretion in the dissemination of truth. The counterargument is sometimes made, "But the Lord doesn't hide! He reveals His beauty in the sunsets, His tender sympathy in the rain, His wrath in the thunder, His restless energy in the brooks, His power in the sunlight."

There are exoteric truths, and there are also esoteric truths. There is that which is revealed impersonally and left up to us to interpret—such as the thunder and our perception of it as divine wrath; the rain and our perception of it as God's sympathy. But behind even God's most open expressions there lies impenetrable mystery.

"The wind blows where it wills," said Jesus in Chapter 3 of the Gospel of St. John. *"You hear the sound of it, but you do not know where it comes from, or where it is going. So is everyone who is born of the Spirit."*

And Sri Krishna says in the ninth Chapter of the
Bhagavad Gita:

> *By Me the whole vast Universe of things*
> *Is spread abroad;—by Me, the Unmanifest!*
> *In Me are all existences contained;*
> *Not I in them!*

God's hidden reality cannot be understood by
the reasoning faculty. India's Shankhya philosophy
states frankly, *"Ishwar ashidha:* God is not prov-
able."

A willingness to seek the underlying reality behind appearances is essential for those who would
know God.

Thus, through holy scripture, God has spoken to
mankind.

Does Satan Exist?

Truth is one and eternal. Realize oneness with it in your deathless Self, within.

The following commentary is based on the teachings of Paramhansa Yogananda.

The Bible tells us in Chapter 4 of the Gospel of St. Matthew:

> *Then [after baptism] was Jesus led up of the spirit into the wilderness to be tempted of the devil.*

To most modern minds, this passage seems quaintly obsolete. Psychologists would say—*have* said, in fact—that the temptation of Jesus, if it occurred at all, was purely psychological. They call it a projection of desires lurking in his own subconscious mind.

The subconscious plays a strong part, certainly, even if not a unique one, in any testing the spiritual seeker must undergo.

The Bhagavad Gita, in dealing with this undeniable reality, quotes Arjuna in the third Chapter, and then Sri Krishna's reply:

*"Yet tell me, Teacher! [said Arjuna] by
what force doth man
Go to his ill, unwilling; as if one
Pushed him in that path?"*

*[Krishna replied:]
"Desire it is!
Passion it is! born of the Darknesses,
Which pusheth him. Mighty of appetite,
Sinful, and strong is this!—man's enemy!"*

Yet even Krishna describes passion as "born of the Darknesses." The fact is, as Paramhansa Yogananda wrote in *Autobiography of a Yogi,* "All thoughts vibrate eternally in the cosmos. . . . Thoughts are universally and not individually rooted; a truth cannot be created, but only perceived." Psychology, yes, but psychology attuned to currents of consciousness that pervade the entire universe, attracted by each of us according to our own personal inclinations.

Yogananda, quoted in *The Path,* said, "I used to think Satan was only a human invention, but now I know, and add my testimony to that of others who lived before me, that Satan is a reality. He is a universal, conscious force whose sole aim is to keep all beings bound to the wheel of delusion."

We should take pains, then, to attract uplifting currents of universal consciousness, and to avoid attracting the negative, which—disease that it is!—can infect our thoughts even while it leads us to believe that our thoughts are purely our own.

Thus, through holy scripture, God has spoken to mankind.

Week 34

How Should We Meet Our Tests?

Truth is one and eternal. Realize oneness with it in your deathless Self, within.

The following commentary is based on the teachings of Paramhansa Yogananda.

Last week we considered Satan's temptation of Jesus in the wilderness, after his baptism by John. We discussed the question, Does Satan exist?

All of us experience temptation of one kind or another in our lives—some of us, frequently; others, only occasionally. Whether temptation comes to us from our own subconscious, or from outside ourselves, is secondary to the fact that it does come, and that we must deal with it. More important, then, is the question, *How* to deal with it—in fact, how to deal with tests of any kind?

Martin Luther flung an ink pot at the devil, who had appeared to test him. A dark stain on the wall of Luther's cell is pointed out to tourists in support of this story. Unfortunately, our trials are not often so summarily dismissed. As a fellow monk once said to Swami Kriyananda, speaking of Satan, "If only I could get my *hands* on him!"

Jesus during his temptations in the wilderness overcame them, and thereby set an example for all time, by clinging the more determinedly to God. As Paramhansa Yogananda used to say, "Darkness cannot be driven out of a room with a stick. Once you turn on the light, however, the darkness will vanish as though it had never been." Jesus manifested this principle. The Bible tells us therefore that at last, *"The devil leaveth him, and, behold, angels came and ministered unto him."*

In the Bhagavad Gita the point is clarified further by the added explanation that there are three qualities in human nature: *sattvic,* or spiritually elevating; *rajasic,* or ego-activating; and *tamasic,* or spiritually darkening. It is this triune aspect of human nature that the third Chapter refers to with the words:

> *As fire is hidden by smoke, as a mirror is dulled by rust, and as an embryo is enclosed in the womb, so is the indwelling Self enveloped by desire.*

Yogananda explained that each of these examples describes one of the qualities, or *guna*s. *Sattva guna,* that which elevates our consciousness, can be freed of any identity with ego by a little puff of meditation and right affirmation. *Rajo guna,* which embroils the ego in restless activity, can be worked off with a little more, and a little longer, effort. *Tamo guna,* embracing as it does such mental states as laziness and stupidity, can only be outgrown in time, since it inhibits even the *desire* for self-improvement.

The example Jesus gave us was intended more for those in whom *sattva guna* is predominant. But if you yourself find elements in your consciousness that resist even the effort to cling to God in prayer and meditation, don't despair. Patience, as it has been well said, is the fastest path to God. As long as your efforts take you steadfastly in the right direction, you will come out right in time. Remember Yogananda's words: "A saint is a sinner who never gave up."

If, however, your nature impels you, even against your will, to move in the wrong direction—toward egoic desires, and away from God—strive at least to detach yourself mentally from your wrong actions, which are induced by habit. The time will come when their own stored-up energy will tire and diminish. At that time, if you have not contributed to that energy by your consenting will, you will find it possible at last to redirect your energies more constructively.

Thus, through holy scripture, God has spoken to mankind.

WHO ARE TRUE CHRISTIANS?

Truth is one and eternal. Realize oneness with it in your deathless Self, within.

The following commentary is based on the teachings of Paramhansa Yogananda.

Jesus Christ said, in Chapter 10 of the Gospel of St. John: *"All that ever came before me are thieves and robbers: but the sheep did not hear them."*

Many Christians, not surprisingly, quote this saying in condemnation of other spiritual teachers—not only the old Testament prophets, but also Buddha, Krishna, and others who lived before Jesus, as well as (by inference) any who came after him. Yet Jesus himself said, in St. Matthew Chapter 5, *"Think not that I am come to destroy the law, or the prophets: I am not come to destroy, but to fulfill."*

Nowhere do we find Jesus condemning, or even gently criticizing, other spiritual masters. His criticisms were reserved for worldly attitudes, and for those hypocritical Pharisees who had allowed religion to become, for them, a pretense.

Paramhansa Yogananda explained that the expression "All that ever came before me" referred to those spiritual teachers who place their egos and their self-importance ahead of the Christ Consciousness, in the sense of drawing people's devotion to themselves and not offering it where alone it truly belongs, to God.

Yogananda himself was very firm in this regard. For example, he never spoke of anyone as his disciple. Instead, he always insisted, "They are God's disciples. God is the Guru, not I."

Ego is a way-station on the soul's journey toward enlightenment. The soul is first trapped in lower bodily forms. Slowly it evolves to the human level, at which point self-consciousness appears. Only in human form can self-consciousness transcend material form altogether, including the lower identity of ego-consciousness, and discover the true, divine Self within. Self-consciousness manifested as ego is an incentive to deliberate self-development. Later in this process of development, however, the ego becomes an obstruction. Inevitably, new spiritual aspirants do not emerge effortlessly from the vortex of ego-consciousness. Desire must be offered up resolutely and ever-more wholeheartedly on the altar of Infinity. It is a gradual process, and few even among those who seek to help others are free of ego. If, however, their motive in teaching is not to serve, but to be served, they deserve a severe reprimand, as Jesus gave them. For their direction of development is no longer upward, but downward. In the name of giving up desires they are creating new ones. As it says in the Bhagavad Gita in the third Chapter:

Desire obscures even the wisdom of the wise. Their relentless foe it is, a flame never quenched.

Intellect, mind, and senses: These combined are referred to as the seat of desire. Desire, through them, deludes and eclipses the discrimination of the embodied soul.

O Arjuna, discipline your senses! And, having done so, work to destroy desire, annihilator of wisdom and of Self-realization.

Give God the credit for everything you do. See Him as the true Doer.

Thus, through holy scripture, God has spoken to mankind.

EGO—FRIEND OR FOE?

Truth is one and eternal. Realize oneness with it in your deathless Self, within.

The following commentary is based on the teachings of Paramhansa Yogananda.

Jesus Christ begins his Beatitudes with the words:

Blessed are the poor in spirit: for theirs is the kingdom of heaven.

To be "poor in spirit" in such a way as to merit the kingdom of heaven doesn't mean to be poor-spirited. Rather, it means to see oneself as owning nothing, since all belongs to God. For all is a manifestation of His consciousness.

St. John of the Cross wrote, "If you would own everything, seek to own nothing." That which the ego relinquishes, offering it up to soul-consciousness, is reclaimed forever in cosmic consciousness. Nothing is ever lost. Paramhansa Yogananda tells the story in *Autobiography of a Yogi* of the levitating saint, Bhaduri Mahasaya.

"Master," said a disciple of this saint once, ardently. "You are wonderful! You have renounced riches and comforts to seek God and teach us wisdom!" It was well-known that Bhaduri Mahasaya had forsaken great family wealth in his early childhood, when single-mindedly he entered the yogic path.

"You are reversing the case!" The saint's face held mild rebuke. "I have left a few paltry rupees, a few petty pleasures, for a cosmic empire of endless bliss. How then have I denied myself anything? I know the joy of sharing the treasure. Is that a sacrifice? The shortsighted worldly folk are verily the real renunciates! They relinquish an unparalleled divine possession for a poor handful of earthly toys!"

The Bhagavad Gita in the third Chapter states:

All things are everywhere by Nature
  wrought
In interaction of the qualities.
The fool, cheated by self, thinks, "This I
  did"
And "That I wrought"; but—ah, thou
  strong-armed prince!—
A better-lessoned mind, knowing the play
Of visible things within the world of sense,
And how the qualities must qualify,
Standeth aloof even from his acts.

Thus, through holy scripture, God has spoken to mankind.

Truth Invites;
It Never Commands

Truth is one and eternal. Realize oneness with it in your deathless Self, within.

The following commentary is based on the teachings of Paramhansa Yogananda.

Free will is a basic principle of life. God never coerces: He *invites* us to live in such a way that we find fulfillment in ourselves. If we refuse to live rightly, Paramhansa Yogananda taught, God simply says, "I will wait." We have eternity to live. In that eternity we live as we choose: in self-created darkness—a darkness as intense, and as long lasting, as we choose—or in the infinite light, the true Self, which is God.

Jesus Christ in the Beatitudes offered a beautiful example of God's way of inviting mankind to seek perfection—not by commanding, but by offering His human children the incentive they need to choose the right of their own volition.

"Blessed are the poor in spirit," Jesus said, *"for theirs is the kingdom of heaven. . . . Blessed are the meek: for they shall in-*

herit the earth. . . . Blessed are the merciful:
for they shall obtain mercy. Blessed are the
pure in heart: for they shall see God."

In each of the Beatitudes Jesus explains the blessing attendant upon observing it. The divine way, similarly, for each of us is not to do violence to our own natures. Spirituality must be attained naturally. It can never be attained by force.

The Bhagavad Gita says, in the third Chapter:

Even the wise behave in accordance with Nature as it is manifested in them. Of what avail, then, is suppression?

The scripture then goes on, however, to explain that this doesn't mean we should surrender to the dictates of our lower nature. Rather, it emphasizes our need to aspire to the heights, but each of us in accordance with *his own* nature and not in imitation of anyone else's, offering ourselves up for purification by divine grace. Desire, whatever form it takes—so the Bhagavad Gita explains—should be resisted, even if only mentally. *"Attachment and repulsion to sense objects, both of these are universally rooted. No one should accept their influence. For, verily, they are man's enemies."*

Thus, through holy scripture, God has spoken to mankind.

Intuition Is Simple: The Intellect Is Complex

Truth is one and eternal. Realize oneness with it in your deathless Self, within.

The following commentary is based on the teachings of Paramhansa Yogananda.

In the Gospel of St. Mark, Chapter 10, we read a passage that Yogananda often quoted:

> *And they brought young children to him, that he should touch them: and his disciples rebuked those that brought them.*
>
> *But when Jesus saw it, he was much displeased, and said unto them, Suffer the little children to come unto me, and forbid them not: for of such is the kingdom of God.*
>
> *Verily I say unto you, Whosoever shall not receive the kingdom of God as a little child, he shall not enter therein.*

It has often been noted that a critical attitude tends to paralyze creativity. Good critics, for example, seldom produce works of creative genius, though their creations may be intellectually clever. The intellect separates; it analyzes, then puts things together again piece by piece. Intellect lacks intuition's flow, which descends smoothly, like a river, from the superconscious.

Paramhansa Yogananda described intuition as "the soul's power of knowing God." To receive the kingdom of God, Jesus was saying, one must do so with the openness and trust of a little child. Intellectuals may object to this statement, saying, "But there must also be discrimination. You wouldn't want a person to be so open-minded that his brain falls out!" The truth is, however, that the intellect can be fooled, even when it does its best to discriminate wisely. Only intuition is capable of penetrating to the heart of a matter and *knowing* truth from falsehood. It was the clear understanding of a child, not the elaborately persuaded intellects of his elders, that enabled the child in Hans Christian Andersen's story to cry out in surprise, "Why isn't the Emperor wearing any clothes?"

Therefore it was that Sri Krishna said, in the ninth Chapter of the Bhagavad Gita:

To you, who are free from the carping spirit, I shall now reveal wisdom sublime. Grasping it with your mind, and perceiving it by intuitive realization, you shall escape the evils of delusion.

Thus, through Holy scripture, God has spoken to mankind.

Week 39

MANY ARE THE PATHWAYS TO TRUTH

Truth is one and eternal. Realize oneness with it in your deathless Self, within.

The following commentary is based on the teachings of Paramhansa Yogananda.

On the dedication page of Swami Kriyananda's book *The Path* appears the following account:

> A group of Paramhansa Yogananda's disciples had gone with him to see a movie about the life of Gyandev, a great saint of medieval India. Afterwards they gathered and listened to the Master explain certain, subtler, aspects of that inspiring story. A young man in the group mentioned another film he had seen years earlier, in India, about the life of Mirabai, a famous woman saint.
>
> "If you'd seen *that* movie," he exclaimed, "you wouldn't even have *liked* this one!"
>
> The Guru rebuked him. "Why make such comparisons? The lives of great saints

manifest in various ways the same, one
God."

The Bible contains a similar account in the Gospel of St. Luke, Chapter 9:

> *And John . . . said, Master, we saw one*
> *casting out devils in thy name; and we for-*
> *bad him, because he followeth not with us.*
> *And Jesus said unto him, Forbid him not:*
> *for he that is not against us is for us.*

The more central a truth, the greater the number
of contexts in which it can be applied. Truth is like
a pure white light, containing within itself the full
spectrum of the rainbow.

Let no one tell you what your path to God *ought*
to be. Many are the paths. Select your own according to the dictates of your own nature, no matter
how out of step that puts you with other people.

Sri Krishna in the third Chapter of the Bhagavad
Gita, states:

> *Trying even unsuccessfully to fulfill one's*
> *own spiritual duty (dharma) is better than*
> *pursuing successfully the duties of others.*
> *Better death itself in the pursuance of one's*
> *own duties. The pursuance of another's du-*
> *ties is fraught with (spiritual) danger.*

Thus, through holy scripture, God has spoken to
mankind.

IN SURRENDER LIES VICTORY!

Truth is one and eternal. Realize oneness with it in your deathless Self, within.

The following commentary is based on the teachings of Paramhansa Yogananda.

A case might be made for surrender as a path to victory in worldly conflicts—the way of passive resistance, for example, in preference to armed resistance. But our point here concerns a higher kind of surrender: the surrender of our deluded, egoic will to the wise and almighty will of God.

Human will is, as Paramhansa Yogananda used to say, guided by whims and limited understanding. The divine will is in harmony with every level of reality. Though the divine will sometimes appears to us, at first, to be wrong, it proves always, eventually, to be for our highest good.

Human will is inconsistent; it leads us one day to success, another, to disaster. The divine will, when we surrender to it completely (though it is not always easy to do so!), always brings us deep inner peace and joy in the end.

Jesus Christ demonstrated this perfect surrender to God's will in the Garden of Gethsemane, the night before he was captured and imprisoned, preparatory to his crucifixion. He went apart from the others to pray, and asked them to pray also. But when he returned to them he found them asleep.

Out of his love for them he excused them, saying, *"The spirit indeed is willing, but the flesh is weak."* He then urged them again, saying, *"Watch and pray."* Their weakness, in those circumstances, was particularly sad, and the disciples themselves must have regretted it bitterly, later on.

We all know the symptoms of human weakness, though we may excuse them in ourselves, saying, "Well, after all, I'm only human." But what are the signs of true strength? We find in all cases that these are the fruit of a life wholly surrendered to God. The Bhagavad Gita lists these signs in the thirteenth Chapter:

> *Humbleness, truthfulness, and harmlessness,*
> *Patience and honor, reverence for the wise,*
> *Purity, constancy, control of self,*
> *Contempt for sense-delights, self-sacrifice,*
> *Perception of the certainty of ill*
> *In birth, old age, and frail mortality,*
> *Disease, the ego's suffering, and sin;*
> *Detachment, lightly holding thoughts of*
>   *home,*
> *Children, and wife—those ties which bind*
>   *most men;*
> *An ever-tranquil heart, heedless of good*
> *Or adverse fortune, with the will upraised*
> *To worship Me alone, unceasingly;*

Loving deep solitude, and shunning noise
Of foolish crowds; calm focus on the Self
Perceived within and in Infinity:
These qualities reveal true Wisdom, Prince.
All that is otherwise is ignorance!

Thus, through holy scripture, God has spoken to mankind.

VICTORY DEMANDS THE COURAGE OF CONVICTION

Truth is one and eternal. Realize oneness with it in your deathless Self, within.

The following commentary is based on the teachings of Paramhansa Yogananda.

Jesus Christ said in the Gospel of St. Matthew, Chapter 10:

> *Think not that I am come to send peace on earth: I came not to send peace, but a sword.*
>
> *For I am come to set a man at variance against his father, and the daughter against her mother, and the daughter-in-law against her mother-in-law.*
>
> *And a man's foes shall be they of his own household.*
>
> *He that loveth father or mother more than me is not worthy of me: and he that loveth son or daughter more than me is not worthy of me.*
>
> *And he that taketh not his cross, and followeth after me, is not worthy of me.*

He that findeth [that is to say, that clingeth to] his life shall lose it: and he that loseth [in other words, that giveth up] his life for my sake shall find it.

God tests the firmness of our faith. The "sword" described here is the sword of discrimination. The struggle Jesus describes is not a war against unknown enemies, but the struggle with our own attachment to all that is nearest and dearest to us, humanly speaking. Ultimately, it is a war against the ego itself, and against anything with which we surround ourselves to bolster the ego's fragile sense of security.

When Yogananda, as a boy, fled to the Himalayas to embrace a life of solitary meditation, he was apprehended by his older brother Ananta, and brought home again. At a certain point, before he would accept defeat, he whispered to his friend Amar, his companion on the flight, "Let us slip away when opportunity offers. We can go on foot to Rishikesh."

But Amar, whose brother had accompanied Ananta, had turned pessimist, disclaiming any intention of continuing their adventure. Yogananda's memorable comment on Amar's refusal was, "He was enjoying the familial warmth."

The spiritual warrior rejects that "familial warmth." Rather, he claims the whole universe as his home.

As the Bhagavad Gita puts it in the fourteenth Chapter:

Unaffected by outward joys and sorrows, or by praise and blame; secure in his divine nature; regarding with equal gaze a clod of mud, a stone, and a bar of gold; impartial toward all experiences, whether pleasant or unpleasant; firm-minded; untouched by either praise or blame; treating everyone alike whether friend or foe; free from the delusion that, in anything he does, he is the doer: Such an one has transcended Nature's triune qualities.

Thus, through holy scripture, God has spoken to mankind.

FIRST THINGS FIRST

Truth is one and eternal. Realize oneness with it in your deathless Self, within.

The following commentary is based on the teachings of Paramhansa Yogananda.

That expression, "First things first," is a piece of counsel often given to students of business techniques. It is the advice of practicality to those who aspire to worldly success. But according to the Hermetic doctrine, "As above, so below," that which works best in one level of life is often the best guide to what will work best on every other level. If a person is true to his highest priorities, he will generally find that his other needs are fulfilled naturally as well.

This is true, certainly, of the search for God. One of the greatest sayings of Jesus Christ was this simple sentence, in the Gospel of St. Matthew, Chapter 6:

> *Seek ye first the kingdom of God, and His righteousness; and all these things shall be added unto you.*

Paramhansa Yogananda gave his elder brother Ananta a wonderful lesson in this truth. It was Ananta who had captured him and brought him back from his flight to the Himalayas, described by Yogananda in *Autobiography of a Yogi*. In Yogananda's book we read how Ananta later challenged him, in the city of Agra, to pit his divine faith against such "practical" worldly considerations as the need for earning a living. Fearless before that challenge, the young aspirant agreed to go by train, without any money, to the nearby town of Brindaban; not to miss a single meal in Brindaban; and to find his way back to Agra without begging and without in any other way asking for help. In one of the most thrilling chapters in the book, Yogananda fulfilled all the conditions of the test. Yogananda continued the account:

> As the tale was unfolded, my brother turned sober, then solemn.
> "The law of demand and supply reaches into subtler realms than I had supposed." Ananta spoke with a spiritual enthusiasm never before noticeable. "I understand for the first time your indifference to the vaults and vulgar accumulations of the world."
> Late as it was, my brother insisted that he receive *diksha* (initiation) into *Kriya Yoga*.

As the Bhagavad Gita puts it in the ninth Chapter:

Those who worship lesser gods go to their gods . . . but those who worship Me come to Me.

Thus, through holy scripture, God has spoken to mankind.

WHAT IS THE BEST WAY
TO PRAY?

Truth is one and eternal. Realize oneness with it in your deathless Self, within.

The following commentary is based on the teachings of Paramhansa Yogananda.

Jesus Christ and Sri Krishna, both, advised praying to God as personal. Yet both emphasized also that God is above form, and that He must be sought, ultimately, in Infinity. As Jesus put it, *"God is a spirit, and they that worship Him must worship Him in spirit and in truth."*

Yet he spoke of God constantly as our Heavenly Father. In what is known as the Lord's Prayer, he proposed a very human prayer to the Heavenly Father, asking fulfillment for all our spiritual needs.

The Bhagavad Gita explains that man, living as he does in a human body, finds it difficult to worship Infinity as though the ego and body didn't even exist. Far better for human beings, Krishna says, to work with reality as we know it than to affirm a reality of which the human mind is incapable of forming any clear notion. Encouraging the devotee in this direction, he says, *"O Arjuna, be thou a yogi!"*—that is to say, be one who works with, not in rejection of, the energies of the body and the natural tendencies of the mind.

In the twelfth Chapter of the Gita, Arjuna asks:

> *"Those who, ever steadfast, worship Thee as devotees [that is to say, in an "I" and "Thou" relationship], and those who contemplate Thee as the immortal, unmanifested Spirit—which group is the better versed in yoga?"*
>
> *The blessed Lord replied: "Those who, fixing their minds on Me, adore Me, ever united to Me through supreme devotion, are in My eyes the perfect knowers of yoga. . . .*
>
> *"Those whose strict aim is union with the Unmanifested choose a more difficult way; arduous for embodied beings is the path of dedication to the Absolute"*—the path, that is to say, of *Gyana Yoga*.

Thus, through holy scripture, God has spoken to mankind.

WHY TELL GOD ANYTHING, WHEN HE KNOWS EVERYTHING?

WHY OFFER GOD ANYTHING, WHEN HE HAS EVERYTHING?

Truth is one and eternal. Realize oneness with it in your deathless Self, within.

The following commentary is based on the teachings of Paramhansa Yogananda.

Jesus Christ teaches as the ideal prayer one that addresses very human demands to God: *"Give us this day our daily bread," "Forgive us our debts, as we forgive our debtors,"* and, *"Lead us not into temptation, but deliver us from evil."*

Jesus himself says, just before suggesting this prayer, *"Your Father knoweth what things ye have need of, before ye ask him."* Why, then, his recommendation that we pray for anything? The answer is that we should *offer ourselves* up in acceptance of His abundance. Don't pester God, as though pulling constantly on His sleeve to get His attention. Approach Him with the confidence of a child in its parent. And in that spirit, then, ask Him lovingly, but with complete trust, as though demanding your birthright, and without the slightest doubt in your mind that He *wants* only your best. For you don't have to persuade Him, the way a beggar or a stranger might. You are His own child.

God knows everything already. He knows what is in your heart. It is *you* who need to clarify your feelings, that you attune yourself to Him in turn more clearly. For only by such clarity will you be able to receive perfectly what He gives you.

For the same reason, we need to offer ourselves to Him not because He needs anything from us (except, as Yogananda said, our love, to complete His love for us), but because by self-giving we expand our awareness from its confinement in the little ego, outward to infinity.

"Those who partake of the nectar remaining after a sacrifice," says the Bhagavad Gita in the fourth Chapter, *"attain to the Infinite Spirit. That person, however, who makes no sacrifices never truly succeeds in enjoying even the blessings of this material world; how, then, could he attain happiness in subtler realms?"*

Thus, through holy scripture, God has spoken to mankind.

FAITH IS A CALL TO PRAYER; PRAYER IS A CALL TO FAITH

Truth is one and eternal. Realize oneness with it in your deathless Self, within.

The following commentary is based on the teachings of Paramhansa Yogananda.

In the Gospel of St. Matthew, Chapters 7 and 21, we read:

> *Ask, and it shall be given you; seek, and ye shall find; knock, and it shall be opened unto you. . . .*
>
> *Verily I say unto you, if you have faith, and doubt not . . . if ye shall say unto this mountain, Be thou removed, and be thou cast into the sea; it shall be done.*
>
> *And all things, whatsoever ye shall ask in prayer, believing, ye shall receive.*

Paramhansa Yogananda showed by his own example that prayer is a power, provided we believe deeply in that power. When our thoughts and feelings are strongly focused and then united in growing awareness to the Divine Presence within, they can bring even seemingly unrealistic wishes to fulfillment.

When Paramhansa Yogananda was in charge of his school in Ranchi, India, he took the boys on occasional outings to the surrounding countryside. "There was a waterfall not far away," he told Swami Kriyananda, "where I took them sometimes. It was dangerous to cross there. But I would cry out to the boys, 'Do you believe in God?' 'Yes!' they would shout back enthusiastically. And so we always crossed in safety.

"Years later, after I'd gone to America, one of the teachers tried to do the same thing, but he lacked spiritual power. One of the boys slipped on a rock and was drowned."

Thus, the Master explained, belief alone is not enough. It must be united to one-pointed awareness, which leads to Self-realization. The Bhagavad Gita, in the sixth Chapter, underscores the necessity for such one-pointed concentration:

> *Whenever the mind, fickle and restless, wanders off from its concentration, let the meditating yogi withdraw it resolutely, spurning every distraction (no matter how alluring!), and bring it back again and again under the control of the Self.*

Thus, through holy scripture, God has spoken to mankind.

Week 46

THE PROMISE OF
THE SCRIPTURES

Truth is one and eternal. Realize oneness with it in your deathless Self, within.

The following commentary is based on the teachings of Paramhansa Yogananda.

In the Gospel of St. Luke, Chapter 15, we read the famous Parable of the Prodigal Son. Jesus tells of the man who took the wealth bestowed on him by his father, and squandered it in foreign lands, where he fell into evil ways. At last, repentant, he returned to his father's home. When his father saw him, he was (Jesus tells us)

> *moved with compassion, and ran and fell upon his neck and kissed him. And the son said to him, "Father, I have sinned against heaven and before thee. I am no longer worthy to be called thy son." But the father said to his servants, "Fetch quickly the best robe and put it on him, and give him a ring for his finger and sandals for his feet; and bring out the fattened calf and kill it, and let us eat and make merry; because this my*

*son was dead, and has come to life again;
he was lost, and is found." And they began
to make merry.*

Small-hearted human beings, identified as they
are with their little egos, give exaggerated importance to any slight they receive from others. Thus,
they imagine God, like them, to be petty, unpardon-
ing, and vindictive. In God's eyes, however, when
human beings go astray there is nothing to forgive.
All of us are aspects, only, of His own Self. He who
made us resides in us. He is not far away from us
in some far-off heaven. His call to us, always, is to
return to our own home, within.

The way of return is described in the Bhagavad
Gita, in the sixth Chapter:

*Supreme blessedness is that yogi's who
has completely calmed his mind, controlled
his ego-active tendencies* (rajas), *and purged
himself of desire, thereby attaining oneness
with Brahma, the Infinite Spirit.*

Thus, through holy scripture, God has spoken to
mankind.

REINCARNATION—
THE SPIRAL STAIRCASE

Truth is one and eternal. Realize oneness with it in your deathless Self, within.

The following commentary is based on the teachings of Paramhansa Yogananda.

In the Book of Revelation, Chapter 3, Jesus Christ tells us:

> *Him that overcometh will I make a pillar*
> *in the temple of my God, and he shall go*
> *no more out.*

There is a difference between Church dogmas, which are based on reasoned deductions from scriptural statements, and the pronouncements of wisdom, which are based on the inner realization of scriptural truths. Reason, like a train, can only follow already-existing tracks of human experience. Human memory, being short, is seldom able to cross back over the threshold of a person's present existence. Biblical references to previous lifetimes on earth are overlooked in the deductive process, and we find them therefore excluded from the body of official dogma. Nevertheless, such references exist. The Bible itself presents them—as does Jesus in this passage—not as abstract teaching, but as direct, personal perception of truth.

In the same way Krishna, in the Bhagavad Gita, silences Arjuna's reasonable doubts on the subject not by reasoned argument, but by the frank statement contained in the fourth Chapter of that great scripture:

> *Arjuna, you and I have passed through many births. I know all of them, though you, O chastiser of foes, recall them not.*

Thus, through holy scripture, God has spoken to mankind.

THE LAW OF KARMA—BONDAGE, OR SOUL-RELEASE

Truth is one and eternal. Realize oneness with it in your deathless Self, within.

The following commentary is based on the teachings of Paramhansa Yogananda.

The Epistle of St. Paul to the Galatians contains this oft-quoted statement:

> *Be not deceived: God is not mocked; for whatsoever a man soweth, that shall he also reap.*

In *Autobiography of a Yogi* Paramhansa tells a story from the life of the Benares saint Trailanga Swami:

> A skeptic once determined to expose Trailanga as a charlatan. A large bucket of calcium-lime mixture, used in whitewashing walls, was placed before the swami.
>
> "Master," the materialist said, in mock reverence, "I have brought you some clabbered milk. Please drink it."

Trailanga unhesitatingly drained, to the last drop, the containerful of burning lime. In a few minutes the evildoer fell to the ground in agony.

"Help, swami, help!" he cried. "I am on fire! Forgive my wicked test!"

The great yogi broke his habitual silence. "Scoffer," he said, "you did not realize when you offered me poison that my life is one with your own. Except for my knowledge that God is present in my stomach, as in every atom of creation, the lime would have killed me. Now that you know the divine meaning of boomerang, never again play tricks on anyone."

The well-purged sinner, healed by Trailanga's words, slunk feebly away.

Yogananda goes on to say:

> The reversal of pain was not due to any volition of the master, but came about through unerring application of the law of justice which upholds creation's farthest swinging orb. Men of God-realization like Trailanga allow the divine law to operate instantaneously; they have banished forever all thwarting crosscurrents of ego.

Not by reason alone, but by Self-realization, are the ins and outs of destiny fully understood. Their web, though tied forever to the post of ego-motivation, is too intricate to be perceived as a single thread. Only great masters can see it with clarity. It is visible to them in all its workings—not from within the tangle, but from above, in superconsciousness.

As Sri Krishna said in the fourth Chapter of the Bhagavad Gita:

He who beholds inaction in action, and action in inaction, is wise among men; he is one with the Spirit; he has attained the true goal of action (perfect freedom).

Thus, through holy scripture, God has spoken to mankind.

What Is It, to Fail Spiritually?

Truth is one and eternal. Realize oneness with it in your deathless Self, within.

The following commentary is based on the teachings of Paramhansa Yogananda.

The first passage is from the Gospel of St. Matthew, Chapter 25. Jesus tells the Parable of the Ten Virgins, five of them wise, and five, foolish. They await their Bridegroom, the Christ Consciousness. The wise virgins keep the oil in their lamps, symbolic of their devotion, lit through the night. The foolish virgins placed no oil in their lamps. These foolish ones are like the average devotee, going through the motions of outer ritual but keeping no fire of love burning in the heart.

When the Bridegroom's coming is announced, the foolish virgins realize their mistake, and hasten out to purchase oil. During their absence, the Christ Consciousness comes and embraces those who have been awaiting him with devotion. The foolish ones, by their lackluster devotion, are not accepted by him. *"Watch, therefore,"* Jesus told his listeners, *"for you know neither the day nor the hour wherein the Son of man cometh."*

In *Autobiography of a Yogi*, Paramhansa Yogananda describes the "foolish virgin" consciousness he encountered in the Mahamandal hermitage he stayed in as a young man, in Benares. "I was pleased," he wrote,

> that my new home possessed an attic, where I managed to spend the dawn and morning hours. The ashram members, knowing little of meditation practices, thought I should employ my whole time in organizational duties. They gave me praise for my afternoon work in their office.
>
> "Don't try to catch God so soon!" This ridicule accompanied one of my early departures toward the attic. . . . [Later, during meditation] I felt lifted as though bodily to a sphere uncircumscribed.
>
> "Thy Master cometh today!" A divine womanly voice came from everywhere and nowhere.
>
> This supernal experience was pierced by a shout from a definite locale. A young priest nicknamed Habu was calling me from the downstairs kitchen.
>
> "Mukunda, enough of meditation! You are needed for an errand."

The Divine Mother's words were not spoken for the benefit of that priest—the "foolish virgin," but for Mukunda, the "wise virgin." For this was the day his guru, Sri Yukteswar, came to him.

Grieve not, friends, if you feel that you have been foolish. No error is forever. Someday, if you keep your lamp lit now, your opportunity will come. In the Bhagavad Gita, the sixth Chapter, Krishna promises every devotee:

> *Arjuna, none who works for self-redemption*
> *Will ever meet an evil destiny!*

Spiritual failure, though a deep disappointment, is always temporary. "Eternal hellfire" is but a projection of vindictiveness in the human mind.

Thus, through holy scripture, God has spoken to mankind.

Week 50

Living in
the Presence of God

Truth is one and eternal. Realize oneness with it
in your deathless Self, within.

The following commentary is based on the teachings of Paramhansa Yogananda.

In the Gospel of St. Matthew, Chapter 25, we
read of a King—capitalized, for the reference is to
God—who welcomes certain devotees to the divine
consciousness, saying, *"I was an hungred, and ye
gave me meat: I was thirsty, and ye gave me drink:
I was a stranger, and ye took me in: Naked, and ye
clothed me: I was sick, and ye visited me: I was in
prison, and ye came unto me."*

The elect asked him when it was they had served
Him in these ways, and the King answered, *"Verily
I say unto you, Inasmuch as ye have done it unto
one of the least of these my brethren, ye have done
it unto me."*

To see God as residing in every human being,
as indeed He does, is to open oneself to limitless
opportunities for serving Him. Paramhansa Yogananda, in *Autobiography of a Yogi*, described a
saint who lived in this consciousness as "the great-

est man of humility I ever knew." He described a seemingly chance encounter with this saint:

> Another day found me walking alone near the Howrah railroad station. I stood for a moment by a temple, silently criticizing a small group of men with drum and cymbals who were violently reciting a chant.
>
> "How undevotionally they use the Lord's divine name in mechanical repetition," I reflected. My gaze was astonished by the rapid approach of Master Mahasaya. "Sir, how come you here?"
>
> The saint, ignoring my question, answered my thought. "Isn't it true, little sir, that the Beloved's name sounds sweet from all lips, ignorant and wise?" He passed his arm around me affectionately; I found myself carried on his magic carpet to the Merciful Presence.

If you would see God, watch for Him everywhere. If you would hear His voice, listen for it in all sounds and also in their supporting silences. If you would know God, seek His wisdom behind merely human knowledge.

The Bhagavad Gita, in the sixth Chapter, states:

> *One who beholds My presence everywhere,*
> *And all things dwelling equally in Me,*
> *He never loses loving sight of Me,*

Nor I of him, through all eternity.

Thus, through holy scripture, God has spoken to mankind.

WHAT WAS
THE STAR OF BETHLEHEM?

Truth is one and eternal. Realize oneness with it in your deathless Self, within.

The following commentary is based on the teachings of Paramhansa Yogananda.

Divine vision is the opposite of worldly sight. Divine vision sees God's presence behind all outward appearances. Worldly sight sees appearances, merely, coating even the blazing wisdom of a saint. A master, to the worldly man, is a human being with, perhaps, a slightly better attitude than the norm. The scriptures therefore strive to demonstrate how the divine consciousness, when openly active among men in the lives of great masters, must never be viewed as an expression of ordinary human consciousness. To seek the presence of Divinity behind the life of a great master is to prepare oneself to recognize that same Divinity also in lower manifestations until at last one beholds God everywhere.

Thus it was that Paramhansa Yogananda, on observing his new disciple Swami Kriyananda struggling with the contrast between the guru's human appearance and his inner, divine reality, looked at him deeply one day and said, "If you only *knew* my consciousness!"

The story of the birth of Jesus Christ contains an account in the Gospel of St. Matthew, Chapter 2, of the star of Bethlehem. The wise men who sought Jesus in his manger said:

> *"We have seen his star in the east." . . .*
> *And, lo, the star, which they saw in the east, went before them, till it came and stood over where the young child was.*

This account was important, for it showed all mankind that Jesus was a divine incarnation, and no ordinary man—that he brought divine consciousness to earth, even though he would play a human role among human beings, and that others, too, by "receiving him" in their inner hearts, would acquire power, as the Bible puts it, to "become the sons of God."

The scriptures enjoin us to meditate on the lives of great souls, that we may discover our own latent spiritual greatness. As the Bhagavad Gita puts it in the fourth Chapter:

> *Who knows the truth touching my births on*
> *   earth*
> *And my divine work, when he quits the*
> *   flesh*
> *Puts on its load no more, falls no more*
> *   down*

To earthly birth: to Me he comes, dear
  Prince!

Thus, through holy scripture, God has spoken to mankind.

Week 52

THE DIVINE ASCENSION

Truth is one and eternal. Realize oneness with it in your deathless Self, within.

The following commentary is based on the teachings of Paramhansa Yogananda.

In the Gospel of St. John, Chapter 14, we read:

> *I am the way, the truth, and the life: no man cometh unto the Father, but by me.*

What is this "I," when spoken by a master who has conquered every vestige of ego-consciousness? Therein lies the mystery of true scriptural teaching. That "I" that is no "I": Does it even exist? In what way is it different from the consciousness that animates other human beings?

Jesus was not saying, "Look at me. Don't look at other masters." He was saying, rather, "Look at the divine Self that is the essence of who you are, your very Self. *You* are that 'I.' No man cometh unto the divine consciousness except by first recognizing his own intrinsic divinity, hidden behind his delusive ego."

The Bhagavad Gita, in the fourth Chapter, states:

O Son of Pritha [Arjuna], in whatever
way people accept Me, in that same way
do I appear to them. For all men, in some
way, pursue the path to Me.

Meditate on the divine incarnations. Their lives, and the consciousness animating them, will be your stairway to the Infinite.

Thus, through Holy scripture, God has spoken to mankind.

THE LAST COMMANDMENT

Truth is one and eternal. Realize oneness with it in your deathless Self, within.

The following commentary is based on the teachings of Paramhansa Yogananda.

Jesus Christ, near the end of the Gospel according to St. John, gave as his last commandment that we love one another.

In John 13:34,35 he said, *"A new commandment I give unto you, That ye love one another; as I have loved you, that ye also love one another. By this shall all men know that ye are my disciples."*

Again in John 15:12 he said, *"This is my commandment, That ye love one another, as I have loved you."*

How did he love us? Personally, yes, in the sense that he loved and forever loves each one of us for who we are, and not abstractly. But impersonally also, in the sense that the Christ, the divine consciousness, is not conscious of itself as separate from us; He loves us not only *for,* but *as,* our very Self. His love is a manifestation of Infinity loving us *as expressions of* infinity. He does not see us as we see ourselves. He forever sees in us our divine potential.

Paramhansa Yogananda made a very similar statement to the monks very shortly before his own departure from his body: "Respect one another, as I respect you." His use of the word, "respect," instead of love, was deliberate. He wanted to emphasize for them the importance of impersonal love and friendship: *from* God, *for* God.

Worldly people do not understand that in impersonal love there is much *deeper* love than exists in personal love. Impersonal love is expansive, not contractive.

One day the Master was going for an outing, and the monks were helping him into his car. Yogananda had been having difficulty with his knees. He remarked, "You all are so kind to me with your many attentions." "Oh, Sir," they replied, "it is *your* kindness to which we respond." The Master smiled sweetly. "God is helping God," he said. "That's His drama."

The second commandment Jesus quoted from the ancient scriptures, *"Love thy neighbor as thy Self,"* explains what he meant by his "new," and last, commandment. We should, he said, love all as reflections of our very Self.

Thus, Paramhansa Yogananda said also, "When I am gone, only love can take my place."

The Bhagavad Gita describes a dialogue between Krishna and his disciple Arjuna. Thus, the other disciples are not part of the scene; the dialogue is internal, and symbolizes the dialogue between the soul and God. Yet in it Sri Krishna describes the way to supreme wisdom, and supreme love: *"The* *serene Self, being one with Brahman, neither grieves nor yearns. **The same to all,** he attains supreme devotion to Me."* (18:54) That sameness toward all is the manifestation of pure love, impersonal in the sense of selfless. By that love, one attains supreme love for God alone.

Thus, through holy scripture, God has spoken to mankind.

About the Author

Swami Kriyananda was a direct disciple of Paramhansa Yogananda, trained by the great Indian master to spread the life-transforming teachings of Kriya Yoga around the globe. He is widely considered one of the world's foremost experts on meditation, yoga, and spiritual practice, having authored nearly 150 books on these subjects.

Kriyananda was the founder of Ananda Sangha, a worldwide organization committed to the dissemination of Yogananda's teachings. In 1968 he founded Ananda World Brotherhood Village, the first spiritual cooperative community based on Yogananda's vision of "world brotherhood colonies." Today Ananda includes ten spiritual communities in the U.S., Europe, and India, and over 140 meditation groups worldwide.

FURTHER EXPLORATIONS

AUTOBIOGRAPHY OF A YOGI
Paramhansa Yogananda

Autobiography of a Yogi is one of the best-selling Eastern philosophy titles of all time, with millions of copies sold, named one of the best and most influential books of the twentieth century. This highly prized reprinting of the original 1946 edition is the only one available free from textual changes made after Yogananda's death. Yogananda was the first yoga master of India whose mission was to live and teach in the West.

In this updated edition are bonus materials, including a last chapter that Yogananda wrote in 1951, without posthumous changes. This new edition also includes the eulogy that Yogananda wrote for Gandhi, and a new foreword and afterword by Swami Kriyananda, one of Yogananda's close, direct disciples.

Also available in unabridged audiobook (MP3) format.

PARAMHANSA YOGANANDA
A Biography with Personal Reflections and Reminiscences
Swami Kriyananda

Paramhansa Yogananda's classic *Autobiography of a Yogi* is more about the saints Yogananda met than about himself—in spite of Yogananda's astonishing accomplishments.

Now, one of Yogananda's few remaining direct disciples relates the untold story of this great spiritual master and world teacher: his teenage miracles, his challenges in coming to America, his national lecture campaigns, his struggles to fulfill his world-changing mission amid incomprehension and painful betrayals, and his ultimate triumphant achievement. Kriyananda's subtle grasp of his guru's inner nature reveals Yogananda's many-sided greatness. Includes many never-before-published anecdotes.

Also available in unabridged audiobook (MP3) format.

THE NEW PATH
My Life with Paramhansa Yogananda
Swami Kriyananda

When Swami Kriyananda discovered *Autobiography of a Yogi* in 1948, he was totally new to Eastern teachings. This is a great advantage to the Western reader, since Kriyananda walks us along the yogic path as he discovers it from the moment of his initiation as a disciple of Yogananda. With winning honesty, humor, and deep insight, he shares his journey on the spiritual path through personal stories and experiences.

Through more than four hundred stories of life with Yogananda, we tune in more deeply to this great master and to the teachings he brought to the West. This book is an ideal complement to *Autobiography of a Yogi*.

Also available in unabridged audiobook (MP3) format.

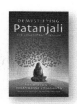

DEMYSTIFYING PATANJALI:
THE YOGA SUTRAS (Aphorisms)
The Wisdom of Paramhansa Yogananda
Presented by his direct disciple, Swami Kriyananda

A great spiritual master of ancient times—Patanjali—en-
lightened humanity through his *Yoga Sutras* with a step-by-
step outline of how all spiritual aspirants achieve union with
God. Since then, scholars have written commentaries that bury Patanjali's
insights in confusing terms. Now, a modern yoga master—Paramhansa
Yogananda—has resurrected Patanjali's original revelations. In *Demysti-
fying Patanjali*, Swami Kriyananda shares Yogananda's crystal clear and
easy-to-grasp explanations.

THE ESSENCE OF THE BHAGAVAD GITA
Explained by Paramhansa Yogananda
As Remembered by his disciple, Swami Kriyananda

Rarely in a lifetime does a new spiritual classic appear that
has the power to change people's lives and transform future
generations. This is such a book.

This revelation of India's best-loved scripture approaches it from a fresh
perspective, showing its deep allegorical meaning and its down-to-earth
practicality. The themes presented are universal: how to achieve victory in
life in union with the divine; how to prepare for life's "final exam," death,
and what happens afterward; how to triumph over all pain and suffering.

Also available in unabridged audiobook (MP3) format.

REVELATIONS OF CHRIST
Proclaimed by Paramhansa Yogananda
Presented by his disciple, Swami Kriyananda

The rising tide of alternative beliefs proves that now, more
than ever, people are yearning for a clear-minded and uplifting understanding of the life and teachings of Jesus Christ.

This galvanizing book, presenting the teachings of Christ from the experience and perspective of Paramhansa Yogananda, one of the greatest spiritual masters of the twentieth century, finally offers the fresh perspective on
Christ's teachings for which the world has been waiting. This book gives
us an opportunity to understand and apply the Scriptures in a more reliable
way than any other: by studying under those saints who have communed
directly, in deep ecstasy, with Christ and God.

Also available in unabridged audiobook (MP3) format.

CONVERSATIONS WITH YOGANANDA
Recorded,with Reflections, by his disciple, Swami Kriyananda

Here is an unparalleled, first-hand account of the teachings of Paramhansa Yogananda. Featuring nearly 500 never-before-released stories, sayings, and insights, this is an extensive, yet eminently accessible treasure trove of wisdom from one of the 20th century's most famous yoga masters. Compiled and edited with commentary by Swami Kriyananda, one of Yogananda's closest direct disciples.

THE ESSENCE OF SELF-REALIZATION
The Wisdom of Paramhansa Yogananda
Recorded, Compiled, and Edited by his disciple,
Swami Kriyananda

With nearly three hundred sayings rich with spiritual wisdom, this book is the fruit of a labor of love. A glance at the table of contents will convince the reader of the vast scope of this work. It offers as complete an explanation of life's true purpose, and of the way to achieve that purpose, as may be found anywhere.

Also available in unabridged audiobook (MP3) format.

WHISPERS FROM ETERNITY
Paramhansa Yogananda
Edited by his disciple, Swami Kriyananda

Many poetic works can inspire, but few, like this one, have the power to change your life. Yogananda was not only a spiritual master, but a master poet, whose verses revealed the hidden divine presence behind even everyday things. This book has the power to rapidly accelerate your spiritual growth, and provides hundreds of delightful ways for you to begin your own conversation with God.

Also available in unabridged audiobook (MP3) format.

~ ~ *The WISDOM of YOGANANDA series* ~ ~

This series features writings of Paramhansa Yogananda not available elsewhere—including many from his earliest years in America—in an approachable, easy-to-read format. The words of the Master are presented with minimal editing, to capture his expansive and compassionate wisdom, his sense of fun, and his practical spiritual guidance.

HOW TO BE HAPPY ALL THE TIME
The Wisdom of Yogananda Series, VOLUME 1, *Paramhansa Yogananda*

Yogananda powerfully explains virtually everything needed to lead a happier, more fulfilling life. Topics include: looking for happiness in the right places; choosing to be happy; tools and techniques for achieving happiness; sharing happiness with others; balancing success and happiness; and many more.

KARMA AND REINCARNATION
The Wisdom of Yogananda Series, VOLUME 2, *Paramhansa Yogananda*

Yogananda reveals the truth behind karma, death, reincarnation, and the afterlife. With clarity and simplicity, he makes the mysterious understandable. Topics include: why we see a world of suffering and inequality; how to handle the challenges in our lives; what happens at death, and after death; and the purpose of reincarnation.

SPIRITUAL RELATIONSHIPS
The Wisdom of Yogananda Series, VOLUME 3, *Paramhansa Yogananda*

This book contains practical guidance and fresh insight on relationships of all types. Topics include: how to cure bad habits that can end true friendship; how to choose the right partner; sex in marriage and how to conceive a spiritual child; problems that arise in marriage; and the Universal Love behind all your relationships.

HOW TO BE A SUCCESS
The Wisdom of Yogananda Series, VOLUME 4, *Paramhansa Yogananda*

This book includes the complete text of *The Attributes of Success*, the original booklet later published as *The Law of Success*. In addition, you will learn how to find your purpose in life, develop habits of success and eradicate habits of failure, develop your will power and magnetism, and thrive in the right job.

HOW HAVE COURAGE, CALMNESS, AND CONFIDENCE
The Wisdom of Yogananda Series, VOLUME 5, *Paramhansa Yogananda*

This book shows you how to transform your life. Dislodge negative thoughts and depression. Uproot fear and thoughts of failure. Cure nervousness and systematically eliminate worry from your life. Overcome anger, sorrow, over-sensitivity, and a host of other troublesome emotional responses; and much more.

HOW TO ACHIEVE GLOWING HEALTH AND VITALITY
The Wisdom of Yogananda Series, VOLUME 6, *Paramhansa Yogananda*

Paramhansa Yogananda, a foremost spiritual teacher of modern times, offers practical, wide-ranging, and fascinating suggestions on how to have more energy and live a radiantly healthy life. The principles in this book promote physical health and all-round well-being, mental clarity, and ease and inspiration in your spiritual life.

Readers will discover the priceless Energization Exercises for rejuvenating the body and mind, the fine art of conscious relaxation, and helpful diet tips for health and beauty.

THE ART AND SCIENCE OF RAJA YOGA
Swami Kriyananda

Contains fourteen lessons in which the original yoga science emerges in all its glory—a proven system for realizing one's spiritual destiny. This is the most comprehensive course available on yoga and meditation today. Over 450 pages of text and photos give you a complete and detailed presentation of yoga postures, yoga philosophy, affirmations, meditation instruction, and breathing practices.

Also included are suggestions for daily yoga routines, information on proper diet, recipes, and alternative healing techniques.

MEDITATION FOR STARTERS *with CD*
Swami Kriyananda

Have you wanted to learn to meditate, but just never got around to it? Or tried "sitting in the silence" only to find yourself too restless to stay more than a few moments? If so, *Meditation for Starters* is just what you've been looking for—and with a companion CD, it provides everything you need to begin a meditation practice.

Filled with easy-to-follow instructions, beautiful guided visualizations, and answers to important questions on meditation, the book includes: what meditation is (and isn't); how to relax your body and prepare yourself for going within; and techniques for interiorizing and focusing the mind.

AWAKEN TO SUPERCONSCIOUSNESS
Swami Kriyananda

This popular guide includes everything you need to know about the philosophy and practice of meditation, and how to apply the meditative mind to resolve common daily conflicts in uncommon, superconscious ways.

Superconsciousness is the hidden mechanism at work behind intuition, spiritual and physical healing, successful problem solving, and finding deep and lasting joy.

LIVING WISELY, LIVING WELL

Swami Kriyananda
Winner of the 2011 International Book Award for
Best Self-Help: Motivational Title

Want to transform your life? Tap into your highest potential?
Get inspired, uplifted, and motivated?

Living Wisely, Living Well contains 366 practical ways to improve your life—a thought for each day of the year. Each reading is warm with wisdom, alive with positive expectation, and provides simple actions that bring profound results. See life with new eyes. Discover hundreds of techniques for self-improvement.

THE RUBAIYAT OF OMAR KHAYYAM EXPLAINED

Paramhansa Yogananda,
Edited by Swami Kriyananda

The *Rubaiyat* is loved by Westerners as a hymn of praise to sensual delights. In the East its quatrains are considered a deep allegory of the soul's romance with God, based solely on the author Omar Khayyam's reputation as a sage and mystic. But for centuries the meaning of this famous poem has remained a mystery. Now Paramhansa Yogananda reveals the secret meaning and the "golden spiritual treasures" hidden behind the *Rubaiyat's* verses—and presents a new scripture to the world.

THE BHAGAVAD GITA

According to Paramhansa Yogananda
Edited by his disciple, Swami Kriyananda

Based on the teachings of Paramhansa Yogananda, this translation of the Gita brings alive the deep spiritual insights and poetic beauty of the famous battlefield dialogue between Krishna and Arjuna. Based on the little-known truth that each character in the Gita represents an aspect of our own being, it expresses with revelatory clarity how to win the struggle within us between the forces of our lower and higher natures.

CRYSTAL CLARITY PUBLISHERS

Crystal Clarity Publishers offers additional resources to assist you in your spiritual journey, including many other books, a wide variety of inspirational and relaxation music composed by Swami Kriyananda, and yoga and meditation videos. To see a complete listing of our products, contact us for a print catalog or see our website: www.crystalclarity.com

Crystal Clarity Publishers
14618 Tyler Foote Rd., Nevada City, CA 95959
TOLL FREE: 800.424.1055 or 530.478.7600 / FAX: 530.478.7610

EMAIL: clarity@crystalclarity.com

ANANDA WORLDWIDE

Ananda Sangha, a worldwide organization founded by Swami Kriyananda, offers spiritual support and resources based on the teachings of Paramhansa Yogananda. There are Ananda spiritual communities in Nevada City, Sacramento, Palo Alto, and Los Angeles, California; Seattle, Washington; Portland and Laurelwood, Oregon; as well as a retreat center and European community in Assisi, Italy, and communities near New Delhi and Pune, India. Ananda supports more than 140 meditation groups worldwide.

For more information about Ananda Sangha communities or meditation groups near you, please call 530.478.7560 or visit www.ananda.org.

THE EXPANDING LIGHT

Ananda's guest retreat, The Expanding Light, offers a varied, year-round schedule of classes and workshops on yoga, meditation, and spiritual practice. You may also come for a relaxed personal renewal, participating in ongoing activities as much or as little as you wish. The beautiful serene mountain setting, supportive staff, and delicious vegetarian food provide an ideal environment for a truly meaningful, spiritual vacation.

*For more information, please call 800.346.5350
or visit www.expandinglight.org*